Amalia's SPECIAL MEXICAN DISHES
Easy and Simple To Prepare

Easy to follow recipes for modern cooking, based on ingredients from your nearest supermarket.

by Amalia Ruiz Clark

NOTE ABOUT THE NEW REVISED EDITION

Since first publication, "Special Mexican Dishes" has been received with great enthusiasm and acceptance. So much so as to excite both the author and publisher to revise and enlarge upon the first edition.

Every attempt has been made to retain this simple style established by the first edition. The revised edition has drawings by the author's grandson and is still printed in the highly readable format without embellishments. It is hoped that we have maintained an original, authentic, highly informative and useful recipe book for the delight of all those who use it and enjoy eating.

PUBLISHED BY:
GILA RIVER DESIGN
P.O. BOX 124
ORACLE, ARIZONA 85623
(602) 896-2395

Cover design by Jacque Keller
Illustrations by Scott Draper & Corel Gallery

Copyright ® 1977 by Amalia Ruiz Clark
Revised edition copyright ®1979 by Amalia Ruiz Clark
New revised edition March 1979, 1985 5th printing
New revised edition November 1994, 6th printing

All rights reserved. No part of this may be reproduced or transmitted in any form or by any means, including photocopying, recording, or by an information storage and retrieval system without permission in writing from the Publisher.

Printed in U.S.A.
ISBN 0-89741-010-6
10 9 8 7 6 5 4 3 2 1

ABOUT THE AUTHOR

Born in Tucson, Arizona, of immigrant parents from Sonora, Mexico, Amalia was reared in a traditional family atmosphere. As the oldest of nine children, she grew up with much responsibility centered around the kitchen. It was in this traditional family environment where she learned to cook firsthand from her mother, helping and experiencing these exciting recipes; thus her appreciation for the joys, smells and trials of traditional Sonoran cooking.

After Amalia married, she continued to please her family with traditional Sonoran cooking. It has been her pleasure to share this rich heritage with others through this cookbook.

Her husband, the late Tom Sr., was her constant source of support and encouragement during the writing of this cookbook. She has two daughters and a son, is a grandmother and great grandmother, and continues to make her home in Oracle, Arizona.

CONTENTS

About the Author iii
Contents iv
Introduction 2
Foods and Ingredients 3
Helpful Hints 3
Chilies 5
Spices 6
Mexican Dishes 7

APERITIVOS (APPETIZERS)
    Aperitivo de Frijol Jalapeño (Jalapeño Bean Dip) 10
    Aperitivo de Frijol (Mexican Bean Dip Fondue) 10
    Aperitivo de Aguacate (Avocado Dip) 11
    Camaron Con Chiles Y Ajos (Chilied Shrimp in Garlic) 11
    Aperitivo Bravo de Aguacate (Peppery Avocado Dip) 12
    Guacamole (Basic Avocado Spread) 12
    Coctel de Abulon (Abalone Cocktail) 13
    Tostada de Queso (Cheese Crisp) 13
    Galletas de Zucchini (Tiny Zucchini Biscuits) 14
    Aperitivo de Jicama Fresca (Fresh Jicama Appetizer) 14
    Jalapeños en Escabeche Rellenos con Queso
        (Pickled Jalapeños Stuffed with Cheese) 15
    Ceveche (Marinated Fish) 16

BEBIDAS (BEVERAGES)
    Chocolate Mexicano (Mexican Chocolate) 18
    Bebida de Pinole (Pinole Drink) 18
    Ponche (Mexican Eggnog) 19
    Chocolate con Kahlua (Chocolate with Kahlua) 19
    Pinole de Trigo (Roasted Ground Wheat Powder) 20
    Sangria (Mexican Party Wine) 20
    Teswin (Fiesta Punch) 21

CARNES Y COMIDAS (MEATS AND SIDE DISHES)
    Asado (Mexican Roast Beef) 23
    Carne Seca (Jerky - Basic Recipe) 23
    Carne Seca Machacada Guisada (Shredded Jerky - Fried) 24
    Carne Seca Machacada con Chile Colorado
        (Shredded Jerky with Chile Sauce) 24
    Carne de Puerco Adobada (Marinated Spiced Pork Loin) 25
    Chuletas de Puerco con Chile Verde
        (Pork Chops with Green Chile) 26
    Burritos Mineros (Miners' Burrito) 26
    Costillas de Puerco Asadas con Salsa de Barbacoa
        (Barbecued Spare Ribs - Pork) 27
    Salsa de Barbacoa (Barbecue Sauce) 27

Burritos de Carne con Chile Verde
(Green Chile Beef Burritos) 28
Chimichangas (Deep Fried Meat Burro) 29
Garnish for Chimichangas 29
Chorizo (Mexican Hot Sausage-Vinegar) 30
Chorizo (Mexican Hot Sausage-Liquor)...................................31
Picadillo (Mexican Hash) 32
Picadillo de Lengua (Beef Tongue Hash).................................33
Guajolote o Gallina con Chile Colorado
(Turkey or Chicken with Red Chile Sauce) 34
Gallina en Pipian (Chicken in Pipian Sauce) 34
Pollo Asado con Arroz (Baked Chicken with Rice)..................35
Relleno de Arroz (Rice Stuffing)..35
Relleno para Guajolote a la Mexicana (Turkey Stuffing, Mexican Style) 36
Torta de Carne Molida (Mexican Meat Loaf) 37
Tortitas de Camaron (Little Shrimp Omelets) 38
Arroz a la Española (Spanish Rice) 39
Macarron con Chile Colorado (Macaroni with Red Chile Sauce) 39
Ejotes con Chile Colorado (Green Beans with Prepared Chile Sauce)............40
Pierna De Carnero A La Mexicana (Leg of Lamb Mexican Style) 40
Corona De Puerco Asada Con Arroz (Roast Crown of Pork with Rice) 41
Huachinango A La Veracruzana (Red Snapper Veracruz Style)....................42
Fajitas En Escabechi De Tequila (Meat Strips Marinated in Tequila) 43
Carne Asada A La Mexicana (Tri-Tip Loin Roast in Chile Marinade) 44

NIXTAMAL
Nixtamal (Mexican Hominy) 45
Nixtamal (Mexican Hominy) 46
Gorditas de Maiz de Masa Fresca (Homemade Corn Tortillas) 46
Gorditas de Maiz de Masa Harina (Homemade Corn Tortillas)...................47
Cucharetas de Tortilla de Maiz (Corn Tortilla Chips) 47
Quesadilla de Tortillas de Maiz (Grilled Cheese Corn Tortilla) 48
Tortillas de Maiz para Tacos (Taco Shells) 48
Tortillas de Maiz para Tacos Blandos (Soft Tacos) 49
Tacos de Carne (Beef Tacos)...49
Ensalada para Tacos (Garnish for Tacos) 50
Variedad de Rellenos para Tacos (Variety of Fillings for Tacos) 50
Tostadas de Frijoles (Bean Tostadas) 51
Chilaquiles (Corn Tortilla Hash)..51
Garnish for Chilaquiles 52
Enchiladas Chatas de Masa Fresca (Flat Enchiladas) 53
Enchiladas Chatas de Masa Harina (Flat Enchiladas) 54
Garnish for Enchiladas 54
Enchiladas de Queso Enrolladas (Rolled Enchiladas Stuffed with Cheese) 55
Enchiladas de Rez Enrolladas (Rolled Beef Enchiladas).........56
Enchiladas Enrolladas con Almendras (Rolled Enchiladas with Almonds) 57
Empanadas Fritas de Masa Fresca (Fried Turnovers) 58

Empanadas Fritas de Masa Harina (Fried Turnovers) 59
Pasta de Chile Colorado (Red Chile Puree) 60
Pasta de Chile Guisado (Prepared Chile Sauce) 60
Chile Con Carne - Guisado (Meat in Red Chile Puree) 61
Chile Colorado con Queso (Red Chile Sauce with Cheese) 61
Mole Poblano (Poblano Sauce) 62
Chile con Carne para Tamales (Chile con Carne for Tamales) 64
Tamales de Chile con Carne de Masa Fresca (Red Chile Beef Tamales) 65
Tamales de Chile con Carne de Masa Harina (Red Chile Beef Tamales) 66
Pastel de Chile con Carne de Masa Fresca (Tamale Pie) 67
Pastel de Chile con Carne de Masa Harina (Tamale Pie) 68
Tamales de Elote (Green Corn Tamales) 68
Pastel de Elote (Green Corn Tamale Pie) 70
Tamales de Frijol de Masa Fresca (Bean Tamales) 71
Tamales de Frijol de Masa Harina (Bean Tamales) 72
Frijoles Pintos (Pinto Beans) (Basic Recipe) 72
Frijoles Fritos (Fried Beans) 73
Frijoles Refritos (Refried Beans) 73
Frijoles Refritos al Horno (Refried Beans - Baked) 73
Frijoles con Carne (Beans with Meat) 74
Frijoles con Chile (Mexican Chile Beans) 74
Frijoles Fritos con Chilies (Beans with Red Chile Peppers) 75
Posole (Beans, Hominy and Pork Hocks) 75
Tortillas de Harina (Flour Tortillas) 76
Tortillas de Harina de Espaura (Flour Tortillas with Baking Powder) 77
Sopapillas (Bread Puffs) 77

SOPAS (SOUPS)
Sopa de Albondigas (Mexican Meat Ball Soup) 79
Sopa de Lentejas (Lentil Soup) 80
Sopa De Frijoles Negro Con Lentejas (Black Been and Lentil Soup) 80
Sopa de Fideo (Vermicelli Soup) 81
Sopa de Pollo (Chicken Soup) 82
Caldo de Queso (Cheese Soup) 83
Casuela de Carne Seca Machacada (Shredded Jerky Soup) 84
Puchero (Mexican Stew) 85
Menudo (Tripe Soup) 86
Sopa De Tortilla (Tortilla Soup) 87

ENSALADAS (SALADS)
Ensalada de Arandano (Cranberry Salad Mold) 89
Ensalada de Fruta Fresca (Fresh Fruit Salad) 90
Ensalada de Papaya y Ciruela (Papaya Plum Salad) 90
Adorno de Crema Agria para Ensalada (Sour Cream Dressing) 91
Ensalada de Aguacate (Avocado Salad) 91
Ensalada de Nopalitos (Nopalitos Salad) 92
Adorno de Vinagre para Ensalada (Vinegar Salad Dressing) 92
Ensalada de Camaron (Shrimp Salad) 93

Ensalada de Papa (Potato Salad) 94
Garnish for Ensalada de Papa 94
Ensalada de Salpicon (Beef Tongue Salad) 95
Ensalada De Noche Buena (Christmas Eve Salada)......96

COMIDAS CON HUEVOS (EGG DISHES)
Huevos Rancheros (Ranch Style Eggs) 98
Huevos a la Benedict en Tortitas de Masa (Eggs Benedict on Masa Patties) 98
Huevos Revueltos con Carne Seca Machacada
  (Eggs Scrambled with Shredded Jerky) 99
Huevos Revueltos con Nopalitos (Scrambled Eggs with Nopalitos)......99
Huevos Revueltos con Chorizo (Scrambled Eggs with Hot Sausage)......100
Huevos Revueltos con Papas (Scrambled Eggs with Potatoes) 100
Huevos Revueltos con Tortillas Tostadas
  (Scrambled Eggs with Tortilla Chips)......101
Tortilla de Huevos con Chile Verde (Green Chile Omelet)......101

SALSAS (HOT SAUCES)
Salsa de Chile Verde (Green Chile Sauce) 103
Salsa Jalapeña (Jalapeño Sauce) 103
Salsa Brava de Chilitos Amarillos
  (Hot Sauce with Yellow Peppers) 104
Salsa de Tomate - Brava (Hot Tomato Sauce) 104
Salsita de Tomate Fresco - Picante (Fresh Tomato Relish - Hot) 105
Salsa Picante de Tomate con Cebolla
  (Hot Tomato Sauce with Onions) 105
Salsa de Jalapeños Encurtidos (Pickled Jalapeño Relish) 106
Pepinillos Bravos (Hot Pickles) 106
Salsa De Fruta (Fruit Salsa) 107

LEGUMBRES (VEGETABLES)
Nopales (Prickly Pear Cactus) 109
Nopales (Prickly Pear Cactus) 110
Nopalitos con Chorizo (Nopalitos with Mexican Sausage) 111
Nopalitos con Chile Colorado (Nopalitos with Red Chile Sauce) 111
Nopalitos con Jamon (Nopalitos with Ham) 112
Nopalitos con Cuajada (Nopalitos with Cottage Cheese) 112
Guisante (Black Eyed Peas) 113
Calabazitas con Elote (Zucchini with White Corn) 113
Spinaca (Spinach) 114
Calabaza Mexicana Cosida (Cooked Mexican Pumpkin) 115
Elote Frito (Fried Corn)......115
Chile Rellenos (Green Chilies Stuffed with Cheese) 116
Chayotes Rellenos (Stuffed Squash)......117

POSTRES (TRADITIONAL SWEETS)
Arroz con Leche (Rice Pudding) 119
Biscochuelos (Pastry - Ring Cookies) 120
Buñuelos (Mexican Crullers) 121
Churros (Mexican Crullers) 122

Miel para Buñuelos (Buñuelo Syrup) 122
Cajeta para Empanadas (Pumpkin Filling for Turnovers) 123
Masa para Empanadas (Pastry for Turnovers) 123
Capirotada (Mexican Bread Pudding) 124
Coyotas (Brown Sugar Pastries) 125
Pastelitos De Boda (Mexican Wedding Cakes) 125
Pastel de Cafe con Datiles y Nueses (Date Nut Coffee Cake) 126
Pastel de Orejones de Albaricoque (Apricot Pic - Dried Apricots) 127
Pasta de Pastel (Pie Crust) 127
Tamalitos de Leche de Masa Fresca
   (Miniature Sweet Corn Masa Balls in Sweet Milk Sauce) 128
Tamalitos de Leche de Masa Harina
   (Miniature Sweet Masa Harina Balls in Sweet Milk Sauce) 129
Flan (Caramel Coated Custard) 130
Flan De Merengue (Meringue Flan) 131
Cajeta de Membrillo (Quince Paste) 132
Jamoncillo (Mexican Fudge) 132
Pepitoria (Pumpkin Seed Candy) 133
Mousse De Kahlua (Kahlua Mousse) 134
Almendrado (Almond Puding) 135
Natilas De Almenrado (Almond Custard) 136
Pan Dulce (Sweet Bread) 137
INDEX 138

INTRODUCTION

Mexican cookery consists of dishes which are native to the country and reflect its history. The ingredients native to Mexico are three basic ones: corn, beans and peppers. However, many new foods and ways of preparing them have been introduced over the years.

The Indians, Mayan and Aztec, cultivated corn, beans and chilies. Dishes, such as tamales and tortillas, were prepared then just as they are today. The metate (pronounced me-tah-te) and the stone pestle, called a metapal, were used to grind the corn to make masa. Today the food chopper is used for the same purpose. The molcajete with the tejolote were used for grinding spices and herbs. The electric blender is the modern method for grinding spices.

Sweet and white potatoes, tomatoes, avocado, pumpkins, pineapple, papayas, vanilla and cocoa beans were also cultivated by the Mayans and Aztecs. Cocoa was used to prepare a special drink which was used for royal and religious purposes, and only men of high ranking status were allowed to drink it. It was much later when the Spaniards introduced new foods, such as sugar, that the chocolate drink became popular all over Europe. Sugar was added to the chocolate drink making it more palatable and delicious than the sour potion of the Aztecs.

The Spaniards brought boat loads of sheep, cattle, chickens, rice and nuts. They also introduced spices such as cinnamon to these people. The use of wine and oil for cooking purposes were new ideas also introduced by the Spaniards.

French cuisine, as well as Austrian and Italian, were introduced in the 1860's during the period that Maximilian of Hasburg reigned over Mexico.

Today the food of Mexico is a blend of Indian, Spanish and other European countries, thus making the Mexican cuisine a delight of contrasts. Mexico has taken the best of these, producing a cuisine with a distinct Mexican character.

Mexican food is complementary to American dishes and they can be served together, not only making delicious eating, but also adding zest and color to your meals.

My wish for you is twofold: that you will enjoy using this easy-to-follow Mexican cookbook, and that your meals will be as exciting and enjoyable as listening to a mariachi band, that is "una comida sabrosa y de colores!"

FOODS AND INGREDIENTS

The foods and ingredients used in these recipes were obtained in supermarkets, gourmet and health food shops, Mexican food grocery stores and tortilla factories. Ready-to-eat fresh corn tortillas and flour tortillas are available at most grocery stores. Also available is Masa Harina, which is dehydrated corn flour, and is a good substitute for fresh masa when fresh masa is not available. There are a few instances where substitutions can be made in ingredients without losing the true Mexican flavor of foods prepared.

The ingredients in the recipes may be increased or reduced, depending on the amount of food to be served. Some recipes may be prepared in large quantities and frozen for later use.

You will find "Helpful Hints" a great aid in your cooking. I recommend that you read the book first to get acquainted with the various foods, ingredients and dishes.

HELPFUL HINTS
Do's and Don'ts:

1. For best flavor - Mexican food should be served hot.
2. For best results - All cooking should be done over low heat, except frying. All stirring should be done with a wooden spoon.

3. To make flour tortillas - Use lard or shortening, but not cooking oil. Use lukewarm water to make dough.

4. To make tamale dough - Use whipped lard or shortening, but not cooking oil. Tamale fillings should be cool.

5. To fry beans - Use lard, bacon drippings or shortening, but not cooking oil.

6. When boiling meat or chicken - Save broth. It can be used for soups and sauces. Cool meat broth can be used in place of water to make tamale dough de Masa Harina.

7. Green chilies - Do place chilies in preheated broiler unit one inch below unit. Turn chilies frequently until they have blistered and browned. When roasted, place chilies in a plastic bag and let stand for 10 minutes. Peel chilies; remove stems if dicing the chilies, leave whole if making chile rellenos. Remove some seeds for a less hot chile. The "hot" flavor of a hot sauce can be altered by using less chilies or adding more tomatoes or tomato sauce to produce a mild hot sauce.

8. To reheat tortillas - Do place the tortilla on an ungreased medium hot griddle. Turn frequently until soft and hot. Place hot tortilla into a bun warmer.

9. If corn tortillas are dry or a little hard - Before heating tortilla, dip palm of your hand in water and rub surface of both sides of tortilla.

10. Dicing onions - Before dicing onions, place onions in freezer for at least 5 minutes. Spread lemon juice on cutting board; onion smell won't be so strong and it will cut down on those tears.

11. Avocado dip and avocado salad - Add lemon juice to retain the color of the avocado.

12. The amount of any spice to be used in cooking can be adjusted to personal taste.

13. Cook garlic cloves slowly when frying and remove cloves before adding other ingredients. Garlic cloves will stay fresh when stored in an airtight jar and refrigerated.

Foods That Can Be Prepared In Advance:
1. Hot sauces, refrigerate.
2. Beans (cooked), refrigerate or freeze.
3. Tortillas (cooked), refrigerate or freeze.
4. Tamales (uncooked), freeze.
5. Enchiladas, freeze.
6. Jerky (strips or shredded), refrigerate or freeze.
7. Meat filling (for burritos and tacos), refrigerate or freeze.
8. Taco shells, refrigerate or freeze.
   freeze.Cheese (grated or shredded),
10. Chile puree, refrigerate or freeze.
11. Green chilies (roasted and peeled), refrigerate or freeze.

CHILIES

Chilies are the ingredients that spell "Mexican food". There is a great variety of chilies, sweet peppery medium hot and hot hot. The tiny ones are the hottest. Chilies are an integral part of many main dishes, as well as the principle ingredients of entrees, appetizers and snacks. Many of the chilies are grown in various parts of the United States; particularly in the states of Arizona, New Mexico, Texas and California. Some are imported from Mexico.

The Anaheim chile is the most commonly used chile in these recipes. It is a mild hot or hot chile. The chile pepper is bright green, 5 to 8 inches long, 1 1/2 to 2 inches in diameter, tapering to a point. The chile pepper in its green stage is known as the "chile verde" and is used in preparing the green chile salsa (salsa de chile verde) and the chilies rellenos. This chile turns a bright red when it ripens. It is picked and strung on loops of string; the length of the loop being about 4 ft. when hung. These are known as "sartas de chile colorado". This chile is aired and left to dry. The red chile is also packaged in bags. Purees and sauces are made from dried peppers through the process of presoaking and grinding. It is also ground in its dry stage to form a chile powder.

The yellow pepper is a small yellow hot pepper about 1 to 1 1/2 inches long and one inch in diameter, which turns a bright red when ripe. Dried pods are ground and used for seasoning. It is used in its yellow stage for fresh sauces, or salsas. This yellow pepper is used in a variety of hot sauces.

The jalapeño pepper is a hot hot, dark green pepper about 2 inches long and 1 inch in diameter. This pepper is usually harvested green and used for fresh relishes or picked and jarred or canned. It is also used for hot sauces.

The chile tepin is a very hot tiny round chile the size of a pea. It is green in color in its fresh stage, and turns red when mature. The chile is harvested and pickled green. Some chile tepines are allowed to mature and are picked red and allowed to dry. It is used mostly in its red dried pepper form to make the hot sauces or crumbled for an individial dish as a seasoning.

Chilies, both fresh and canned, red dried chile pods, pastes, purees, sauces, chile powder and a variety of bottled hot sauces are available at most grocery stores and supermarkets. The canned chilies come labeled mild to hot, very hot, pickled hot, minced or whole.

The hottest part of the chile is the seed. Remove seeds for a mild hot flavor and rinse in cold water. Wash hands thoroughly after handling chilies or wear gloves.

SPICES

Oregano: Is marjoram. The leaf is left to dry. It is powdered or crushed. It is stored in jars or cellophane bags.

Cilantro: Fresh coriander leaves, also known as Chinese parsley. The seed is gathered when ripe, dried, ground and stored in jars or cellophane bags. Fresh coriander is found in the produce departments of supermarkets.

Anise: The seed is gathered when ripe, dried, ground and stored in jars or cellophane bags.

Panocha or Piloncillo: Is unrefined brown Mexican sugar. It is sold in small cone shaped loaves and is found in the spice sections of Mexican grocery stores. Dark brown sugar may be substituted (see recipes) if unable to obtain panocha.

Mexican chocolate: An instant chocolate Mexicano with sugar and spices. It comes in round blocks divided into sections. To make chocolate drink follow instructions on the package. It is found in some supermarkets. Unsweetened cocoa may be subsituted (see recipes) if unable to obtain Mexican chocolate.

MEXICAN DISHES

Tortillas: A thin, round pancake-like wafer, made with wheat flour dough or ground corn "masa".

Burrito: A flour tortilla with your favorite filling, such as beans, meats, or scrambled eggs, rolled in tube-like fashion with one end folded up to keep stuffing from falling out.

Chimichanga: A burrito, with both ends folded, fried crisp and topped with hot sauce.

Taco: A corn tortilla fried crisp in a "U" shape filled with a variety of fillings and garnished with lettuce and hot sauce.

Tostada: A crisp flat flour or corn tortilla. Flour tortilla is browned in oven with butter, or topped with grated melted cheese and thin green chile strips. Corn tortilla crisp is spread with guacamole or piled high with any filling, such as beans, cheese, meats, chorizo and shredded lettuce.

Guacamole: Mashed avocado with blends of herbs, onions and seasoning.

Tamale: Masa jacket: Corn dough which is spread on a corn husk with a filling in the center, such as chile con carne or sweet bean mix. The prepared corn husk is then shaped around the filling in burrito style and steam cooked.

Enchilada: Rolled - A corn tortilla with any of a variety of fillings, such as cheese, onions, or meats, rolled burrito style, and covered with a special chile sauce. Flat - A flat "masa" enchilada patty, deep fried, then covered with special chile sauce and garnished with grated cheese, shredded lettuce, chopped olives and onions.

Chile Rellenos: Green chilies, roasted peeled, stuffed with cheese strips, dipped in an egg batter and fried till golden brown.

Chorizo: A highly seasoned sausage.

APERITIVOS

(Appetizers)

APERITISO DE FRIJOL CON CHILE JALAPEÑO
JALAPEÑO BEAN DIP

- 2 cups refried beans (see recipe or canned)
- 1 cup sour cream
- 1 pickled jalapeño chile (minced)

Combine ingredients, mix thoroughly and refrigerate. Use with corn chips, potato chips or any snack crackers. (Yields 1 1/2-2 cups)

APERITIVO DE FRIJOL
MEXICAN BEAN DIP FONDUE

- 4 cups Refried Beans (see recipe, or canned)
- 1 cup chopped green chiles (roasted an peeled or canned)
- 1 large onion (minced)
- 2 fresh tomatoes (minced)
- 1 tablespoon Tabasco Sauce
- 1/2 teaspoon garlic powder
- 2 tablespoons bacon drippings
- 1/2 pound grated cheese (sharp Cheddar), save 1/2 cup
- 1/2 pound jack cheese (grated)

Combine all ingredients, except cheese, in a crock pot and cook at low heat for 3 hours. Add cheese and cook for 1 hour on low. Place in a fondue dish and sprinkle 1/2 cup Cheddar cheese. Serve hot. Use your favorite chips with this dip. (Yields 5 cups)

APERITIVO DE AGUACATE
AVOCADO DIP

1	8-ounce package cream cheese
1/2 pint	sour cream
dash	garlic powder
1/2 teaspoon	salt
1	large ripe avocado
1/4 cup	green onion (finely chopped)
1/8 teaspoon	Tabasco Sauce
1 tablespoon	lemon juice

Allow cream cheese to soften at room temperature. Combine cream cheese, sour cream, garlic and salt in blender and blend.

Peel, pit and cut up avocado. Blend avocado in blender and remove to mixing bowl. Add green onion and Tabasco Sauce and mix well. Add lemon juice and mix thoroughly. Chill at least 2 hours prior to use. Use favorite chips or crackers with dip. (Makes 3 cups)

CAMARÓN CON CHILES Y AJOS
CHILIED SHRIMP IN GARLIC

1 pound	shrimp cooked, deveined and shelled
1 cup	extra light olive oil
	Juice of 3 limes or lemons
4 tablespoons	vinegar from pickled jalapeños
1/2 teaspoon	crushed oregano
12	garlic cloves crushed
12	pickled jalapeños, sliced

Place marinade in a glass bowl, add shrimp and marinate for 3 hours. Drain shrimp. Arrange shrimp on a bed of lettuce on a platter and garnish with pickled slices of jalapeño. (Serves 12)

APERITIVO BRAVO DE AGUACATE
PEPPERY AVOCADO DIP

2	ripe avocados (peeled, pitted and mashed)
1/2 cup	mayonnaise or salad dressing
1/4 cup	green onion (finely chopped)
1/4 teaspoon	salt
1/8 teaspoon	garlic powder
1/8 teaspoon	cayenne red pepper
1 teaspoon	lemon juice

Mix ingredients, adding each ingredient in order. Mix thoroughly or blend briskly in blender. Pour into a bowl, cover and refrigerate. (Yields approx. 1 pint)

GUACAMOLE
BASIC AVOCADO SPREAD

2	ripe avocados
dash	of garlic powder
1/2 teaspoon	salt
1/4 cup	green onion (minced)
1 teaspoon	lemon juice

Peel and pit avocados. Place avocados, garlic powder and salt in blender and blend. Remove from blender to mixing bowl. Add green onion and lemon juice and mix thoroughly. Cover bowl and refrigerate prior to use.

Use as basic spread on toasted corn tortillas (tostadas). May also be used as dip. (Spreads 6 tostadas)

COCTEL DE ABULÓN
ABALONE COCKTAIL

1	16-oz. can whole abalone
1 cup	abalone juice
1	large lemon (juice only)
1	4 1/2-oz. can ripe olives (chopped)
2	8-oz. cans peas (very young early small peas) (LeSueur brand peas)
1	16-oz. can French style green beans
1	24-oz. can tomato sauce
1 cup	tomato juice
3	pickled jalapeño peppers (finely diced)
1/4 cup	liquid from jalapeños

Dice abalone, marinate in lemon juice one hour. Drain peas; set aside. Drain string beans and cut into strips 1" long. Add to abalone and lemon juice, the peas, olives, green beans, jalapeños, tomato sauce, tomato juice, jalapeño liquid and abalone liquid. Chill 3 to 4 hours before serving. (Yields 2 quarts)

TOSTADA DE QUESO
CHEESE CRISP

12	tortillas (flour or corn)
1 pound	cheese (jack or Cheddar, grated)
1/4 pound	butter (melted)

Brush each tortilla very lightly with butter and place flat on baking sheet. Place in oven and heat at 400° for about 2 - 3 minutes (do not brown). Remove and spread grated cheese over each tortilla. Return to oven and bake about 10-15 minutes or until tortilla is golden brown and cheese has melted and bubbles. (Yields 12 tostadas)

GALLETAS DE ZUCCHINI
TINY ZUCCHINI BISCUITS

2 cups	grated zucchini (uncooked)
1/2 cup	flour
1 teaspoon	baking powder
1	egg
1/8 teaspoon	salt
1 tablespoon	sugar

Combine sifted flour, baking powder and grated zucchini in a bowl. Beat egg, salt and sugar together and add to zucchini mixture. Mix well. Grease a cookie sheet and drop batter one tablespoonful at a time. Bake in a preheated oven at 400° for 20 minutes or until golden brown. Serve as a snack or appetizer, with soups, Picadillo, Ensalada de Salpicon; plain, or with butter or cheese. (Yields 2 1/2 dozen)

APERITIVO DE JICAMA FRESCA
FRESH JICAMA APPETIZER

30	Jicama slices
	lemon or lime juice
	salt to season
1/2 cup	chile powder

Cut Jicama slices with different shaped cookie cutters for a variety of slices. Squeeze lemon juice and sprinkle salt on Jicama slices. Arrange Jicama slices on a platter and set beside bowl of chile powder. Dip Jicama slice in the chile powder. Jicama slices can also be used with a dip.

NOTE: Jicama is a crisp root vegetable. It can be obtained in the produce department of some supermarkets. (Yields 30 slices)

COPYRIGHT AMALIA RUIZ CLARK, 1986

JALAPEÑOS EN ESCABECHE RELLENOS CON QUESO
PICKLED JALAPEÑOS STUFFED WITH CHEESE

24	chile jalapeños (pickled canned)
1/2 cup	cooking oil or shortening
1 cup	grated cheese (Cheddar)
1/2 cup	saltine cracker crumbs (12)
2	eggs (beaten)
2 tablespoons	milk

Cut slit in jalapeño chile, take seeds out and leave the stem. Rinse in cold water. Stuff chiles with grated cheese. Set aside.

TO MAKE BATTER: Combine cracker crumbs and flour in a plastic bag and shake to mix thoroughly. Beat eggs with milk. Roll stuffed chile in cracker crumb flour, then dip in egg milk batter, again roll in cracker crumb flour.

TO FRY: Heat oil in skillet and fry chiles until golden brown. Place on absorbent paper and let cool. Arrange on platter. These little stuffed chiles make an excellent appetizer.

NOTE: Canned pickled jalapeños can be bought at most supermarkets. This chile is very hot. Taking seeds out and rinsing chile in cold water decreases the hotness. (Yields 24 chiles)

CEVECHE
MARINATED FISH

2 pounds	mackerel, red snapper, or sea bass fillets
2 cups	fresh lime juice
1 cup	extra virgin olive oil
4	garlic cloves, minced, saute in oil and discard garlic
2 pounds	fresh tomatoes, peel, remove seeds and chop
1/2 cup	tomatoe ketchup
1/3 cup	fresh cilantro, chopped
1 tablespoon	Tobasco sauce
1/8 teaspoon	dry oregano
1/2 teaspoon	salt
1/2 teaspoon	freshly ground pepper
1	jalapeño, minced
1/2 cup	chopped green olives
1/8 cup	capers
10	whole pitted olives for garnish

Place fish in a glass bowl; pour in lime juice, cover and marinate for 2 1/2 hours, refrigerate. Heat oil in skillet, add garlic and saute for 3 minutes. Discard garlic and let the oil cool. In a large glass bowl place oil and next 11 ingredients. Drain fish and rinse with cold water. Add fish to tomatoe mixture. Adjust seasoning to taste. Serve in cocktail glasses. Garnish with whole pitted olives, lime wedges and serve with crackers or bread. This marinade can be used with shrimp and scallops. (Serves 10)

COPYRIGHT AMALIA RUIZ CLARK, 1986

BEBIDAS

(Beverages)

CHOCOLATE MEXICANO
MEXICAN CHOCOLATE

2 tablespoons	unsweetened cocoa
4 tablespoons	sugar
dash	of salt
2 tablespoons	water
1 stick	cinnamon
2 cups	milk
1/8 teaspoon	vanilla

Combine cocoa, sugar, salt, water and cinnamon stick in a saucepan. Boil and stir for 2 minutes or until cocoa dissolves. Add milk and stir constantly over low flame until mixture reaches boiling point. DO NOT BOIL. Remove from heat, add vanilla and beat with a rotary beater until frothy. A favorite pastry to serve with chocolate is Churros. (Serves 2)

BEBIDA DE PINOLE
PINOLE DRINK

3 tablespoons	pinole
8 ounces	milk (hot or cold)
1 teaspoon	sugar
1/4 teaspoon	ground anise

Combine and stir all ingredients in a glass for a drink of pinole.

NOTE: Prepared wheat or corn pinole powder ready for drinks can be bought at Mexican market. Wheat grains can be bought at health food stores. (Yields 1 - 8oz. drink)

PONCHE
MEXICAN EGGNOG

4	egg whites
4	egg yolks (slightly beaten)
2 cups	milk
1/3 cup	sugar
1/4 cup	wine or brandy
	optional: nutmeg or cinnamon

Beat egg whites until stiff. Add slightly beaten egg yolks and beat quickly to retain as much firmness as possible.

Quickly heat the milk and add the sugar. Add to egg fluff and beat quickly. Add wine or brandy and beat briskly. Garnish with a sprinkle of cinnamon or nutmeg. Pour into hot mugs. (Serves 4)

CHOCOLATE CON KAHLUA
CHOCOLATE WITH KAHLUA

2 tablespoons	unsweetened cocoa
3 tablespoons	sugar
1 stick	cinnamon
2 cups	half and half (fresh cream and milk)
4 tablespoons	Kahlua liqueur

Combine cocoa, sugar, water and cinnamon stick in a saucepan. Boil and stir for 2 minutes or until cocoa dissolves. Add half and half fresh cream and stir constantly over low flame until mixture reaches boiling point. DO NOT BOIL. Remove from heat, add Kahlua liqueur and beat with a rotary beater until frothy.

PINOLE DE TRIGO
ROASTED GROUND WHEAT POWDER

    1 pound   whole wheat grains
    2 quarts   water

Wash wheat grains in several waters. Place wheat grains in a large saucepan, add water and boil for 15 minutes. Drain wheat grains and spread out in a shallow baking pan. Let wheat grains dry for a day.

Roast the dry wheat grains in a preheated oven at 475° for about 7 to 10 minutes, turning grains constantly for even browning.

TO MAKE PINOLE: grind the roasted wheat grains in a food grinder using a fine blade. Grind into a fine powder.

TO MAKE PINOLE DRINK: Follow recipe on following page. (Yields 1/2 pint)

SANGRIA
MEXICAN PARTY WINE

    16 ounces   dry red wine chilled
    1 cup   brandy
    1/2 cup   sugar
    1 cup   pinneapple juice
    1 cup   orange juice
    1   lime, thinly sliced
    1   lemon, thinly sliced
    1   orange, thinly sliced

Stir all ingredients in a large pitcher and refrigerate for no more than 1 hour, or peels will make wine taste bitter. Serve wine in large wine goblets over ice. (Serves 10)

Copyright Amalia Ruiz Clark, 1986

TESWIN
FIESTA PUNCH

2 lbs.	white dry corn
3 1/2 lbs.	sugar
1/2 lb.	panocha (crushed)
1 - 4oz. package	yeast
3	orange peelings (dry)
1 1/2 tablespoons	anise (coarsely ground)
1 1/2 tablespoons	cloves (coarsely ground)
4 sticks	cinnamon (3 inches)
3.25 gallons	water (cold)
1 - 5 gallon	crock (to make teswin)

Roast corn in preheated oven 350° for 15 minutes turning constantly until light brown. Let cool, grind very coarse with a food chopper: wash in several waters, discard hulls. Drain, place into crock and add sugar, panocha, yeast, orange peelings, and cinnamon sticks. In a square clean white cloth 8 x 8 put anise and cloves, bring ends together and tie with string. Place in crock and add water. Stir with a long wooden spoon and cover with a clean cloth 30 x 45 tying it around crock. Set aside away from drafts.

DO NOT DISTURB. Test teswin on the 7th day using a dry glass container. If teswin is too sweet let it stand (2) more days only, then strain using a paper coffee filter, into glass gallons. Store teswin in a cool place like you would wine. Five gallon crocks usually available at feed or hardware stores.

NOTE: A delightfully pleasing light corn wine enjoyed for centuries during any fiesta time. This popular slightly sparkling punch resembles the pungent drinks made by the country farmers of Southern France and Northern Spain yet it retains a captivating flavor which only it's Northern Sonoran heritage can give it. (Yields 3 gallons)

COPYRIGHT AMALIA RUIZ CLARK, 1986

CARNES Y COMIDAS

(MEATS AND SIDE DISHES)

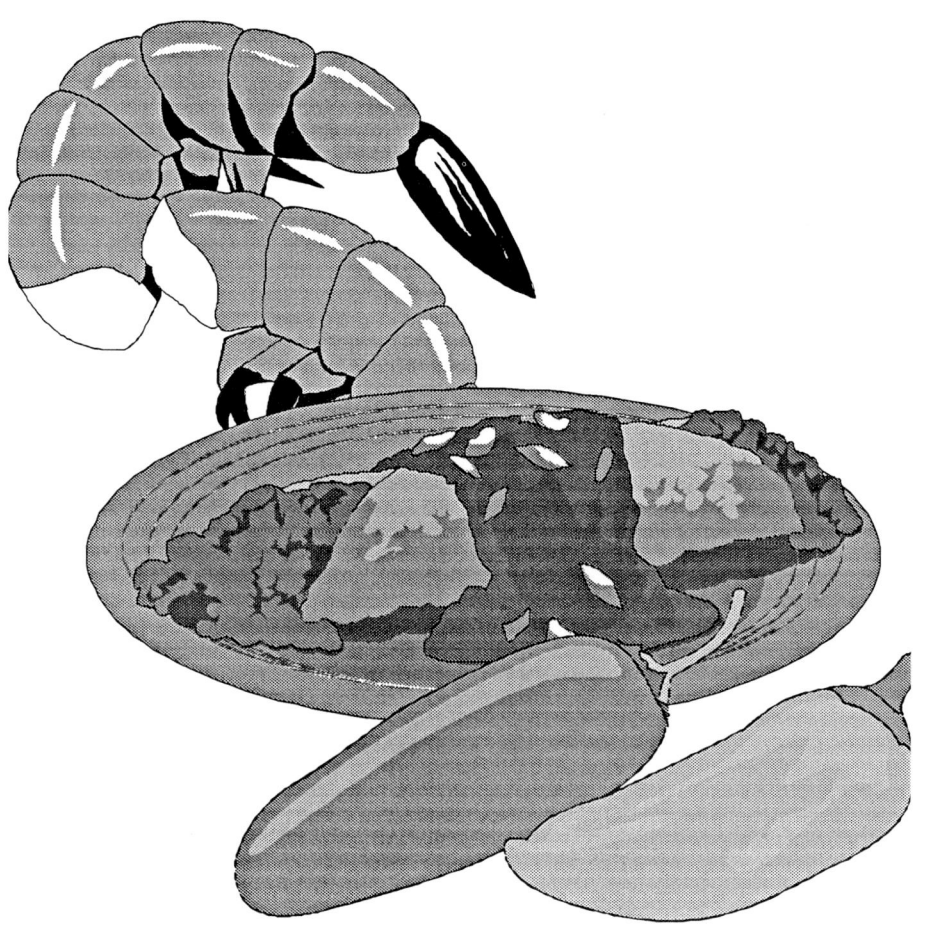

Copyright Amalia Ruiz Clark, 1986

ASADO
MEXICAN ROAST BEEF

2 pounds	round beef steak 2 inches thick
3 tablespoons	lard or shortening
1 cup	flour
1 clove	garlic (chopped)
3	tomatoes (cubed)
3	green chiles (cut in half lengthwise)
2	onions (cut into thick slices)
1 teaspoon	salt
1 teaspoon	black pepper (cracked)
2 1/2 cups	hot water

Pound flour into steak until all flour is used and season. Heat lard in a skillet and brown the steak on both sides in very hot lard. Add ingredients and water. Transfer to a casserole, cover and bake at 350° until tender (approximately 1 1/2 hours) (Serves 6)

CARNE SECA
JERKY BASIC RECIPE

4	round steaks
	salt
	pepper
	garlic powder
	liquid smoke (optional)

Cut strips across the grain of steak into 6 or 8 inch strips, about 1 inch wide. Salt and pepper the strips thoroughly, and season lightly with garlic powder. Hang on a wire line to dry inside a screened, ventilated, sunny area for 2 days. Bake in a pan in preheated oven at 275° for 20 minutes, turning strips over once while baking. Allow to cool and store in a paper bag. Jerky is ready to eat. Will freeze.

For a spicy jerky, do not season with garlic powder. Use liquid smoke instead, brushing each strip with the liquid.

Copyright Amalia Ruiz Clark, 1986

CARNE SECA MACHACADA GUISADA
SHREDDED JERKY - FRIED

2 cups	shredded jerky
2 tablespoons	shortening
2 tablespoons	flour
1/2 cup	green chiles (roasted, peeled, and chopped or canned)
1	fresh tomato (chopped) or 1/3 cup canned tomato
1/2 cup	green onions (chopped)
1/4 teaspoon	salt
1/2 cup	water

Heat shortening in a pan, add flour and brown lightly. Add chiles, tomatoes, onions and shredded jerky. Mix thoroughly. Add the water and simmer 15 minutes.

TO SHRED JERKY: Soak in hot water for 20 minutes, drain, put one cup at a time in blender and shred. (Serves 2)

CARNE SECA MACHACADA CON CHILE COLORADO
SHREDDED JERKY WITH CHILE SAUCE

1½ tablespoons	cooking oil
1	medium potato (cubed)
¼ teaspoon	salt
2 cups	shredded jerky
2 cups	Prepared Red Chile Sauce (see basic recipe)

Heat shortening in saucepan. Add cubed potatoes and salt. Cover pan and cook over low heat for 15 minutes, turning potatoes over two or three times. Do not brown. Add jerky and mix thoroughly. Add Prepared Red Chile Sauce and simmer 15 minutes. Serve hot. (Serves 4)

Copyright Amalia Ruiz Clark, 1986

CARNE DE PUERCO ADOBADA
MARINATED SPICED PORK LOIN

2 pounds	pork loin
24	dry red chiles
4	garlic cloves
1/2 to 2/3 cup	water
2 teaspoons	salt
1 teaspoon	white vinegar
1 teaspoon	oregano

Cut pork loin into thin strips 5 to 6 inches long and about 2 inches wide. Place in a deep dish and set aside. Wash and clean the dry peppers, leaving a few seeds in for spicy flavor. Place the clean chile peppers in a large pot and add enough hot water to cover all the chiles. Cover the pot and soak the chiles for 30 minutes. Save 2/3 cup water to make chile pulp. Place following ingredients in a blender: drained chiles, garlic cloves, salt, water and vinegar. Blend mixture to form a pulp. Add oregano to the pulp and mix. Add this pulp mixture to the meat, soaking all the strips. Marinate overnight. Take strips and hang to dry in a cool ventilated place, just like you would for beef jerky. Roast dry strips of meat in preheated oven at 275° for 25 minutes.

Freshly marinated strips of meat can be fried or roasted. Only a little shortening should be used to fry the pork over a low flame. Fry crisp until well done, or roast in preheated oven at 275°. Roast 35 minutes, or until well done. (Serves 6)

CHULETAS DE PUERCO CON CHILE VERDE
PORK CHOPS WITH GREEN CHILE

6	pork chops
1 teaspoon	salt
1/2 teaspoon	black pepper
1/4 cup	flour
1 tablespoon	cooking oil
1 cup	canned tomatoes
1 cup	green chiles (roasted, peeled and chopped; or canned)
1/2 cup	onion chopped

Season and dredge chops with flour. Heat oil in skillet, brown both sides of chops lightly. Add tomatoes, green chiles, and onion. Cover and simmer 30 minutes, or until tender. (Serves 4 to 6)

BURRITO MINERO
MINERS' BURRITO

4	flour tortillas (12" in diameter)
2 cups	Carne Seca Machacada Guisada (see recipe page 21)

TO PREPARE BURRITOS: Follow same procedure as recipe Burritos De Carne Con Chile Verde.

These burritos are "Miners'" lunch box favorites. (Yields 4)

COSTILLAS DE PUERCO ASADAS CON SALSA DE BARBACOA
BARBECUED SPARE RIBS-PORK

3-4 pounds	spare ribs (cut in 4 inch pieces)
1 tablespoon	salt
1/8 teaspoon	garlic powder
4 cups	water
	Barbecue Sauce (see following recipe)

Sprinkle salt and garlic powder on the ribs and place in a roaster. Add the water, cover the roaster and bake in a preheated oven at 350° for 1 1/2 hour until tender. Uncover and brush barbecue sauce on ribs. Baste with the sauce for 1/2 hour more in the oven.

These ribs can also be barbecued on an outdoor grill. Turn ribs often on the grill, basting each time. Cooking time approximately 1 hour. (Serves 6 or 8)

SALSA DE BARBACOA
BARBECUE SAUCE

1 quart	catsup
1 small can	El Pato brand tomatoe sauce
1/4 cup	brown sugar
1/3 cup	sugar
1/2 cup	wine vinegar
1 tablespoon	salt
1 teaspoon	white pepper
1 teaspoon	garlic powder
1 teaspoon	crushed red peper
1/8 teaspoon	sage
1/2 cup	Coca Cola

Combine all ingredients. Mix well. Prepare this barbecue sauce in advance.

Copyright Amalia Ruiz Clark, 1986

BURRITOS DE CARNE CON CHILE VERDE
GREEN CHILE BEEF BURRITOS

2 pounds	cooked roast or pork (cubed to make 4 cups)
1 1/4 cups	broth (thickened gravy)
1	medium onion (finely chopped)
1 cup	diced green chiles (roasted and peeled or canned)
1	fresh tomato (chopped)
1 teaspoon	salt
1/2 teaspoon	black pepper
1/8 teaspoon	garlic powder
12	flour tortillas (approximately 10-12 inches in diameter)

Place diced meat in saucepan. Add all remaining ingredients and mix well. Heat and simmer 15 minutes to cook in flavor, stirring frequently.

TO PREPARE BURRITO: Spoon 4 tablespoons of filling down center of tortilla. Roll tortilla tube-like, one end folded up to keep filling from falling out. (Yields approx. 12 burros)

CHIMICHANGAS
DEEP FRIED MEAT BURRO

12	flour tortillas (12" in diameter)
1 1/2 pounds	ground beef
1 teaspoon	salt
1/2 teaspoon	black pepper
1/4 teaspoon	garlic powder
1 cup	cooking oil or shortening (for deep frying)
1/2 cup	diced green chiles (roasted, peeled and chopped or canned)

Fry meat in skillet (use 2 tablespoons oil). Separate meat and brown, season with salt and pepper to taste. Add garlic, onion and green chiles. Set aside.

TO PREPARE CHIMICHANGA: Follow the same preparation as recipe for Burritos De Carne Con Chile Verde, but fold both ends of burrito and fasten loose edge with wooden toothpicks. Prepare 2 or 3 tortilla burros at a time. Deep fry in hot shortening or cooking oil, turning until golden brown. Use tongs to remove the browned chimichangas and place on a thick layer of paper towels. Allow excess fat to drain. Keep in warm place until ready to serve.

NOTE: Filling may be varied with shredded chicken, shredded pork, roast beef, chile con carne, refried beans, ect.

GARNISH FOR CHIMICHANGAS

1/2 cup shredded cheese 2 cups shredded lettuce 1 cup chopped radishes Garnish with shredded cheese, shredded lettuce and radishes.

COPYRIGHT AMALIA RUIZ CLARK, 1986

CHORIZO
MEXICAN HOT SAUSAGE VINEGAR

5 pounds	ground beef or 2 1/2 pounds ground beef and 2 1/2 pounds ground pork
1 cup	white vinegar
4 teaspoons	salt
1 tablespoon	oregano
1	head (8 cloves) garlic (crushed)
1	8-oz. package red chile powder
1 1/2 quarts	red chile puree

Mix vinegar and meat thoroughly. Add salt, oregano and crushed garlic. Add the red chile powder gradually, kneading it into the meat mixture until all chile powder has been used up. Add the red chile puree to the mixture and knead it in. Allow mixture to marinate for one hour, then drain excess liquid, if any. Refrigerate or freeze until ready to use.

TO COOK: Fry in skillet using low flame for about 15 minutes. Stir frequently to insure even cooking. Frying may be done without shortening. If shortening is needed, use sparingly. One cup of chorizo makes two servings.

SUGGESTIONS FOR SERVING: With eggs, refried beans, or mixed with fried potatoes. (Yields approx. 4 quarts of chorizo)

CHORIZO
MEXICAN HOT SAUSAGE
TEQUILA - LIQUOR

1 1/2 pounds	ground beef
1 1/2 pounds	ground pork
8	cloves garlic (crushed)
3 teaspoons	salt
1 tablespoon	oregano
1/3 cup	Tequila
8 ounces	chile powder
3 cups	chile puree

Combine ground meat, garlic and seasonings and mix thoroughly. Allow stand 1 hour. Add 1 cup Tequila, mix thoroughly and marinate 1 hour. Add chile powder and chile puree. Mix thoroughy and place in a covered bowl. Marinate overnight for a rich flavor.

This chorizo is as delicious as chorizo prepared with vinegar, but with slightly different flavor because of the use of Tequila in place of vinegar.

To cook: use same cooking directions as for the chorizo with vinegar. Refrigerate or freeze. (yields 3 pints)

COPYRIGHT AMALIA RUIZ CLARK, 1986

PICADILLO
MEXICAN HASH

1 pound	ground meat
1 tablespoon	cooking oil
1	clove garlic
1	potato (cubed)
1	onion (minced)
1 teaspoon	salt
1/2 teaspoon	black pepper
1 teaspoon	cloves coarsely ground
1/2 cup	seedless raisins
1/2 cup	green olives (chopped)
1/2 cup	canned tomatoes
1/2 cup	water

Fry garlic clove in oil. Remove garlic clove; place meat, onions, potatoes and seasonings in same oil. Cook 5 minutes. Add remaining ingredients. Mix well and simmer for 25 minutes.

This Picadillo is an excellent filling for burritos, tacos and chimichangas. (Serves 4 to 6)

COPYRIGHT AMALIA RUIZ CLARK, 1986

PICADILLO DE LENGUA
BEEF TONGUE HASH

2 cups	cooked tongue (diced)
1 tablespoon	cooking oil
1 cup	chopped onion
1 cup	green chile (roasted, peeled and chopped; or canned)
3/4 teaspoon	salt
1/4 teaspoon	black pepper
dash	of garlic powder

Heat oil in a saucepan. Sauté onion and green chile. Add beef tongue, salt, pepper and garlic powder. Mix thoroughly. Cover and simmer for 15 minutes. (Serves 4)

GUAJOLOTE O GALLINA CON CHILE COLORADO
TURKEY OR CHICKEN WITH RED CHILE SAUCE

1 cup	cooked turkey or chicken
3 cups	Prepared Red Chile Sauce (basic recipe)
1/2 teaspoon	oregano

Place red chile sauce in a quart-size pan and bring to a boil. Add the turkey or chicken and oregano. Simmer for 15 minutes, stirring occasionally.

Serve hot. (Serves 4)

GALLINA EN PIPIAN
CHICKEN IN PIPIÁN SAUCE

1 three-pound	chicken (cooked, boned, skinned and cut in bite size pieces)
1 cup	broth
3 cups	chile puree
1 cup	pumpkin seeds (shelled, toasted)
1/2 cup	roasted peanuts
3 tablespoons	lard or shortening
1 1/4 teaspoons	salt

Use electric blender to grind pumpkin seeds and peanuts. Add 1 cup broth. Add puree to mixture and mix thoroughly. Heat lard in saucepan, add mixture and simmer 15 minutes, stirring constantly until the mixture thickens. Add salt last because mixture might curdle if the salt is added sooner. Add cooked chicken and continue to simmer 20 minutes longer.

NOTE: Shelled pumpkin seeds can be obtained at most health food stores. (Serves 6)

POLLO ASADO CON ARROZ
BAKED CHICKEN WITH RICE

1	three-pound whole fryer
1 tablespoon	oil
	salt,
	pepper
	garlic powder

Rub oil on the fryer, inside cavity and out. Sprinkle salt, pepper and garlic powder. Place in a large casserole, cover and bake in preheated oven at 350° for 25 minutes. Uncover and stuff it with Relleno De Arroz (see recipe following page). Place remaining rice around it and bake uncovered for 15 minutes or until brown. (Serves 6)

RELLENO DE ARROZ
RICE STUFFING

1 cup	rice
1 tablespoon	shortening
2 1/2 cups	hot water
1 cube	of chicken bouillon
1/2 cup	green chile (minced)
1/2 cup	green onions (minced)

Heat shortening in a saucepan. Add rice and brown lightly. Dissolve bouillon in hot water and add to rice. Cover tightly and cook over low heat for 20 minutes. Uncover, add chiles and onion. Mix lightly. Stuff fryer.

Copyright Amalia Ruiz Clark, 1986

RELLENO PARA GUAJOLOTE A LA MEXICANA
TURKEY STUFFING, MEXICAN STYLE

1/2 pound	butter
1	medium potato (diced)
1 cup	celery (diced)
1/4 cup	finely chopped onion
1/3 cup	green olives (chopped)
1/2 cup	raisins
1	banana (thinly sliced)
1	apple (diced)
1	fresh green chile (finely chopped)
1/4 teaspoon	black pepper
1/4 teaspoon	ginger
1/4 teaspoon	ground cloves
1	6-oz. bag bread dressing (turkey giblets cooked and minced)
3 cups	broth (from cooked giblets)

Cook giblets in a saucepan in 6 cups water and 1/4 teaspoon salt for 1 hour or until tender. Save about 4 cups broth. Mince cooked giblets and set aside.

Melt butter in a large pot on low heat. Combine all ingredients except bread stuffing and saute in melted butter. Add bread stuffing and mix thoroughly. Pour the hot broth over mixture and toss lightly. Stuff turkey. Excess stuffing may be baked separately. (Yields stuffing for 10 or 12 pound turkey)

TORTA DE CARNE MOLIDA
MEXICAN MEAT LOAF

2 pounds	ground meat
1 cup	medium crunched saltine crackers (20 crackers)
2	beaten eggs
1 cup	dairy sour cream or 1 8-oz. carton
1/2 cup	chopped green chile peppers (roasted and peeled or canned)
2	chopped green onions and tops
1 teaspoon	salt
1/4 teaspoon	garlic powder
2 teaspoons	chile powder (for garnish)

Combine all ingredients (except chile powder), mix thoroughly. Place into 9x5x3 inch loaf pan. Bake in preheated oven at 350° for 1 1/2 hours. Remove from oven, let stand 10 minutes, drain excess fat. Transfer meat loaf to platter and sprinkle chile powder in zigzag pattern on top. (Serves 8)

TORTITAS DE CAMARÓN
LITTLE SHRIMP OMELETS

4	egg yolks
4	egg whites
3 tablespoons	minced onion
2 tablespoons	coriander (fresh chopped cilantro)
2 tablespoons	flour
1/4 teaspoon	salt
1/2 ounce	ground dried shrimp
6 tablespoons	shortening
4 cups	Prepared Red Chile Sauce

Beat egg whites with electric beater until stiff. Fold in flour and salt. Add slightly beaten egg yolks. Fold in shrimp, onion and coriander to mixture.

Heat shortening in skillet. Using tablespoon measure, drop mixture by spoonfuls into hot shortening. Each tablespoonful will make one patty about two inches in diameter. Cook patties until golden brown on both sides. Remove from skillet and set aside on paper towel to drain. Yields about 30 patties.

Heat chile sauce in a saucepan until it comes to a boil. Add shrimp patties, lower the heat, and simmer for 15 minutes.

Shrimp patties may be eaten plain. This is a delicious lenten dish. (Serves 6 to 8)

ARROZ A LA ESPAÑOLA
SPANISH RICE

1 cup	white rice
1/4 cup	shortening
1/2	onion (chopped)
1	fresh medium tomato (chopped) or substitute 1/2 cup canned tomato
2 1/4 cups	hot water with 2 bouillon cubes, beef or chicken (or natural broth seasoned with salt to taste)

Melt shortening in saucepan. Add rice and brown lightly. Add onion and sauté. Add tomatoes and mix well. Add liquid and seasoning and bring to a boil. Transfer mixture into casserole, cover and bake in preheated oven at 300° for 30 minutes.

MACARRÓN CON CHILE COLORADO
MACARONI WITH RED CHILE SAUCE

4 cups	cooked macaroni (drained)
2 cups	Prepared Red Chile Sauce (see basic recipe)
1 cup	grated cheese, cheddar or Colby
1/2 head	lettuee (shredded)
1/2 cup	chopped radishes
2	green onions and stems (chopped)
1/2 cup	green olives (chopped)

Heat the Prepared Red Chile Sauce in a saucepan. Add cooked macaroni and bring to a boil. Simmer for 5 minutes. Add the cheese and simmer 3 or 4 minutes more, or until cheese is melted. Place in a casserole and garnish with lettuce, radishes, green onions and olives. Serve hot. (Serves 6)

Copyright Amalia Ruiz Clark, 1986

EJOTES CON CHILE COLORADO
GREEN BEANS WITH PREPARED RED CHILE SAUCE

2 cups	green string beans (cooked and drained)
2 cups	Prepared Red Chile Sauce (see basic recipe)

Heat Prepared Red Chile Sauce in a saucepan. Add string beans and simmer for 10 minutes. Serve hot. (Serves 4)

PIERNA DE CARNERO A LA MEXICANA
LEG OF LAMB MEXICAN STYLE

1	leg of lamb, trim all fat
4	garlic cloves, mashed
2 tablespoon	chile powder
2 tablespoon	water
	Salt and freshly ground pepper
2 tablespoon	cider vinegar
3 tablespoon	extra virgin olive oil

Mash garlic and add oregano. Mix chile powder with water. Mix all ingredients to make a paste. With a sharp pointed knife make incisions in the leg of lamb and fill with the paste. Whisk vinegar and oil together with seasonings and pour over lamb and let stand overnight. Roast at 400 degrees for 15 minutes, lower temperature and cook at 350 degrees, uncovered. Allow 30 minutes cooking time per pound. (Serves 12)

Copyright Amalia Ruiz Clark, 1986

CORONA DE PUERCO ASADA CON ARROZ
ROAST CROWN OF PORK WITH RICE

16 pork ribs, in a single slab, ask your butcher to trim and tie into crown.

MARINADE

1/2 cup	light soy sauce
1 cup	orange juice
1/4 cup	lime juice
1 tablespoon	Tabasco
1 teaspoon	sugar
1/2	teaspoon salt
5	garlic cloves minced

Blend all ingredients in a food processor. Pour marinade over crown of pork. Marinate pork for 3 hours. Place roast crown of pork in a baking pan. Bake ribs in a preheated oven at 450° F for 15 minutes. Lower temperature to 350° F and bake ribs for 2 hours, basting regularly with marinade. Fill the center with cooked wild rice. Garnish with crushed red pepper. (Serves 8)

Suggestion: Serve with fruit salsa , see recipe page 107.

HUACHINANGO A LA VERACRUZANA
RED SNAPPER VERACRUZ STYLE

2 pounds	red snapper or other fish fillets
4	limes
1 teaspoon	salt
1 teaspoon	pepper
1	large onion (chopped)
3	garlic cloves (minced)
2 pounds	fresh tomatoes (peeled and chopped)
2 tablespoon	capers (drained)
1 cup	spanish green olives (pitted and chopped)
1	jalapeño chile (sliced thin)
1/4 cup	olive oil

Squeeze lime juice over fish - both sides, sprinkle with salt and pepper. Set aside while preparing sauce.

SAUCE: Sauté onions and garlic in moderate hot oil in a large sauce pan. Add tomatoes, capers, olives and jalapeño chile. Season to taste. Simmer 10 minutes. Place fish fillets in single layer in a buttered baking pan. Pour sauce over fish, bake in a preheated oven at 350 ° for 20 or 25 minutes or until fish flakes when tested with fork. Do not overbake. Serves 6.

Note:
Arroz A La Espanola (Spanish Rice) may be served with fish.

FAJITAS EN ESCABECHI DE TEQUILA
MEAT STRIPS MARINATED IN TEQUILA

2	pounds skirt meat or sirloin tip
1/4	cup tequila
1/4	cup fresh lime juice
1	garlic clove (mashed)
1/2	teaspoon black pepper - dash of salt
1	large onion (sliced thin)
1/2	cup white vinegar or cider vinegar
1/4	cup water

Cut meat in 3 inches long 1/4 inch thin strips. Mix tequila and lime juice. Add garlic, pepper, and salt. Place meat and tequila mixture in a glass or stainless steel bowl. Marinate meat for 2 hours, turning meat once or twice. Mix vinegar and water; add onion slices and marinate 1 hour. Pan broil Fajitas in a hot skillet coated with 1 tablespoon of cooking oil, turning meat over twice (2 or 3 minutes cooking time). Place on a hot platter. In same skillet sauté drained onions for 2 minutes. Place onions around meat. Serves 6.

Suggestions ~

To serve Fajitas burrito style; Fill middle of a flour tortilla with Fajitas and onions then fold tortilla and garnish with your favorite salsa.

For a special drink: Margaritas or your favorite beer.

CARNE ASADA A LA MEXICANA
TRI-TIP LOIN ROAST IN CHILE MARINADE

2 pounds	Tri-Tip Loin Roast

Marinade

1/4 cup	orange juice, fresh
2 tablespoons	HomMade Chile Sauce
2 tablespoons	chile powder, Gebhart Original
2 tablespoons	soy sauce
2 tablespoons	light virgin olive oil
1 teaspoon sugar	
1 teaspoon	grated orange peel
2 cloves	garlic, mashed
1/2 teaspoon	salt
1/2 teaspoon	tabasco sauce
1 medium	orange sliced thinly
1/4 cup	fresh cilantro, cut up

Combine marinade ingredients and whisk thoroughly. Place meat and marinade into a large Ziplock plastic bag and marinate meat for 3 or 4 hours.

Grill meat over medium heat, brushing some of the marinade on meat from time to time. (Serves 6)

Salsa De Fruta goes well with this dish.

This marinade can also be used for flank-brisket and pork loin.

NIXTAMAL

(MEXICAN HOMINY)

Mexican hominy is corn kernels that have been dried, husked and shelled. These are then soaked in lime water and cooked until the hulls become separated or can be rubbed off. The corn is then rinsed in cold water. This hulled soft corn is the "Nixtamal" (hominy), which is used in various soups, such as menudo and posole. It is also ground, to make fresh masa, which is used to make corn tortillas and various dishes, such as flat enchiladas and tamales. Because of the time involved in preparing nixtamal and fresh masa, both can be bought already prepared in a tortilla factory or most Mexican markets. Here are some recipes using nixtamal (hominy) and corn tortillas. If you are unable to get fresh masa, try "Masa Harina", which is made by the Quaker Oats Company.

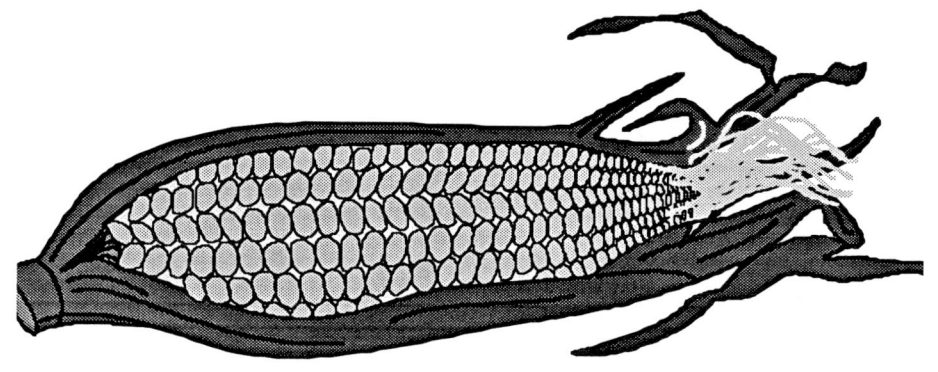

NIXTAMAL
MEXICAN HOMINY

3 pounds	husked and shelled white corn
3 quarts	cold water
3 ounces	hydrated (slaked) lime

Place corn in a large pot, cover with cold water, add the lime and dissolve it. Bring the corn to a boil. Reduce heat to keep water hot, but do not boil. Stir constantly until corn begins to peel. Remove from fire and let cool. Rub the kernels between the hands until the hulls separate. Discard hulls and rinse corn well in cold water. This soft hulled corn is the nixtamal. To make fresh masa, place hulled corn in food chopper and grind using "fine" blade. (Yields 6 pounds of masa)

GORDITAS DE MAIZ DE MASA FRESCA
HOMEMADE CORN TORTILLAS

1 pound	fresh masa
1 tablespoon	water (if masa is dry)

Work the water into the masa. Knead until well blended. Divide into 12 parts the size of a golf ball. Place ball between wet hands and with palms pat the dough to form thin tortilla about 5 or 6 inches in diameter. It can also be done by pressing the ball of masa between two pieces of wax paper. Cook the patty on a lightly greased griddle using medium heat. Both sides should be a light brown when cooked. Serve hot as a snack with butter or cheese, as an appetizer, or with any Mexican dish. (Yileds 12)

GORDITAS DE MASA HARINA
HOMEMADE CORN TORTILLAS

    2 cups   Masa Harina
1 1/4 cup   water

Combine Masa Harina, water. Knead well. Divide masa dough into 12 balls the size of a golf ball.
TO PREPARE AND COOK: Follow instructions in recipe for Gorditas De Maiz De Masa Fresca. (Yields 12)

CUCHARETAS DE TORTILLA DE MAIZ
CORN TORTILLA CHIPS

  12   corn tortillas
1 cup   lard or shortening
        salt

Cut stacked tortillas into four to eight wedges. Heat lard in saucepan or skillet. Fry a few tortilla pieces at one time until golden brown and crisp. Drain on a paper towel. Salt while still warm. Repeat process until all pieces are fried.
SERVE with any of the chile sauces and dips.

QUESADILLAS DE TORTILLAS DE MAIZ
GRILLED CHEESE CORN TORTILLAS

12	corn tortillas
1 pound	grated jack or Cheddar cheese
1 cup	green chiles (roasted, peeled and chopped or canned)
1/4 cup	onions (chopped)
1/2 cup	ripe olives (chopped)

Lay tortilla flat on baking sheet using 6 tortillas. Sprinkle cheese lightly over each tortilla. Add chopped green chile, onion and olives sparingly and evenly. Sprinkle a little more cheese, then cover each prepared tortilla with another tortilla. Bake in preheated oven at 400° for about 10 minutes, or until slightly browned. (Yields 6 Quesadillas)

TORTILLAS DE MAIZ PARA TACOS
TACO SHELLS

12	corn tortillas
2 cups	lard

Heat lard in a deep fryer or saucepan. Fry one tortilla at a time in very hot lard. Fry tortilla open for a few seconds to get it started, then fold it in half keeping it slightly open with the tongs, to allow room for the filling. Fry untill crisp and golden brown on both sides. Taco shells can be prepared and frozen for later use.

TORTILLAS DE MAIZ PARA TACOS BLANDOS
SOFT TACOS

Dip corn tortillas, one at a time in hot lard for a few seconds. Place on paper towels and drain or blot excess fat. Fill the tortilla with any of your favorite fillings. Fold in half and garnish.

See garnish recipe.

TACOS DE CARNE
BEEF TACOS

12	corn tortillas
2 cups	lard
1 pound	ground beef
1/4 cup	water
1 teaspoon	salt
1/2 teaspoon	black pepper
1/2 teaspoon	garlic powder

Combine ground beef, seasonings and water. Mix well. Spread 2 tablespoons of meat on 1/2 of the tortilla using all the meat equally on all the tortillas. Set aside. Heat lard in a deep fryer or saucepan. Fry one filled taco at a time. Fry open for a few seconds then fold it in half. During frying, hold it slightly open with tongs to provide room for garnishing. Fry until crisp and golden brown. Garnish (see recipe following page). (Yields 12 tacos)

ENSALADA PARA TACOS
GARNISH FOR TACOS

1/2 head	lettuce (shredded)
1/2 pound	Cheddar cheese (grated)
1/2 cup	radishes chopped (optional)
1 pint	Salsa De Tomate Brava (see recipe)
1	8 1/2-oz. canned peas combined with prepared hot sauce

Take prepared taco, garnish with cheese, 1 or 2 tablespoonful of salsa, lettuce and radishes. (Garnish for 12 tacos)

VARIEDAD DE RELLENOS PARA TACOS
VARIETY OF FILLINGS FOR TACOS

2 cups	cooked chicken (shredded)
2 cups	cooked pork (shredded)
2 cups	Picadallo (see recipe)
2 cups	cooked roast beef (shredded)
2 cups	cooked mixed chorizo with beans

TOSTADAS DE FRIJOLES
BEAN TOSTADAS

12	corn tortillas
6 tablespoons	lard (or cooking oil)
2 cups	fried beans (refer to fried bean recipe)
1/2 pound	grated cheese (Colby or Longhorn)
1/2 head	lettuce (shredded)
1 cup	diced radishes
	Hot Tomato Sauce (see basic recipe)

Fry each tortilla flat, one by one, in the lard or oil until golden brown and very crisp. Drain on paper towels and place on a baking sheet. Spread 2 tablespoons of heated fried beans on each tortilla and sprinkle with cheese. Garnish with shredded lettuce and radishes. Top with hot tomato sauce for zest as desired.

VARIATION: Top the bean tostada with fried chorizo. Omit the hot sauce. (Yields 12 tostadas)

CHILAQUILES
CORN TORTILLA HASH

12	corn tortillas (cut in small strips) dry, stale or left over tortillas are best
1/3 cup	lard or shortening
1/3 cup	Cheddar cheese (cubed)
4 cups	chile puree
1 teaspoon	salt

Heat lard in a skillet. Add cut up tortillas and fry until crisp and light brown, turning frequently. Add 4 cups, chile puree with salt. Mix thoroughly, reduce heat and simmer 10 minutes. Add 1/3 cup cubed cheese. Stir twice and place in a casserole. Bake in preheated oven at 350° for 25 minutes. Chilaquiles can be frozen. (Serves 4)

GARNISH FOR CHILAQUILES

1/2 cup	shredded cheese (Cheddar or Longhorn)
1/2 cup	onions (minced)
1/2 cup	green olives (minced)
1/2 head	lettuce (shredded)
1/2 cup	radishes (minced)

Garnish with shredded cheese, onions, lettuce, olives and radishes.

COPYRIGHT AMALIA RUIZ CLARK, 1986

ENCHILADAS CHATAS DE MASA FRESCA
FLAT ENCHILADAS

4 cups	masa fresca
1/2 teaspoon	salt
1/4 cup	water
1 cup	cheese, shredded (longhorn or Colby)
1 cup	lard or cooking oil (for deep frying)
5 cups	Prepared Red Chile Sauce (see basic recipe)

Mix masa, water, salt and cheese. Mix well. Divide masa into 12 balls the size of a tennis ball.

TO MAKE MASA PATTY: Flatten the masa ball forming a patty about 3 1/2 to 4 inches in diameter and about 1/4 inch thick. Fry in deep lard or oil until crisp or golden brown on both sides. Remove from skillet and allow to drain on paper towels. Set aside.

TO PREPARE ENCHILADAS: Heat the Prepared Red Chile Sauce, reduce heat and maintain at simmering point. Place 2 or 3 fried masa patties at a time into the simmering chile sauce; allow to soak 2 or 3 minutes, remove soaked patties and place them on a large platter. Continue until all patties have been used. Pour remaining sauce over them and then garnish.

Enchiladas (without garnish) may be stored in freezer until ready to use.

TO GARNISH ENCIiILADAS: Follow instructions on following page. (Serves 6)

ENCHILADAS CHATAS DE MASA HARINA
FLAT ENCHILADAS

2 cups	Masa Harina
1 1/2 cups	water
1/2 teaspoon	salt
1/2 cup	shredded cheese (Longhorn or Colby)
1 cup	lard or cooking oil (for deep frying)
3 cups	Prepared Red Chile Sauce (see basic recipe)

Mix masa, water, salt and cheese. Mix well. Divide Masa Harina dough into 8 balls the size of a tennis ball.

TO MAKE MASA PATTY AND PREPARE ENCHILADAS: Follow the same preparation and garnish for recipe for Enchiladas Chatas De Masa Fresca. (Serves 4)

GARNISH FOR ENCHILADAS

1 cup	Colby cheese, grated
1/2 cup	green olives, chopped
1/3 cup	green onions, chopped
1 cup	diced radishes
2 cups	lettuce, shredded

Sprinkle cheese over soaked patties first, then olives, green onions, lettuce and radishes.

Do not freeze this. (Garnish for 12 enchilada,)

ENCHILADAS DE QUESO ENROLLADAS
ROLLED ENCHILADAS STUFFED WITH CHEESE

12	corn tortillas
1 cup	oil or shortening (for dipping tortillas)
1 pound	grated cheese (Colby or longhorn)
4 cups	Prepared Red Chile Sauce (Use basic recipe)
1/2 head	lettuce (shredded)
1 cup	green olives (chopped)
2 cups	green onions (chopped)
1 cup	radishes (chopped)

TO PREPARE ROLLED ENCHILADAS: Follow the same preparation as recipe for Enchiladas De Rez Enrolladas substituting cheese filling for meat filling. Garnish with shredded lettuce, chopped olives, green onions and radishes.

Enchiladas may be frozen without garnish. (Serves 6)

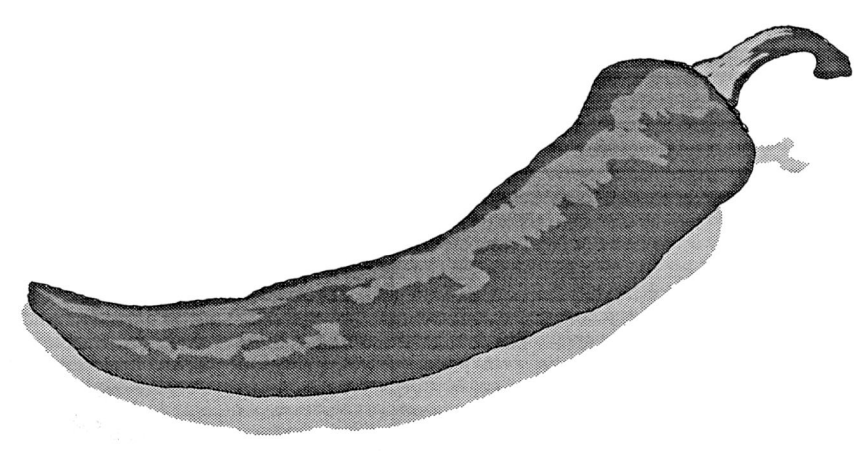

ENCHILADAS DE REZ ENROLLAIDS
ROLLED BEEF ENCHILADS

12	corn tortillas
1 cup	oil or shortening for frying tortillas
1 pound	ground beef
1/4 teaspoon	garlic powder
1/2 teaspoon	salt (to taste)
1/2 cup	chopped onion
1 1/2 cups	shredded cheese (Colby or Cheddar)
4 cups	Prepared Red Chile Sauce (see basic recipe)
1/2 head	shredded lettuce
1 pint	sour cream

Heat oil in a saucepan. Combine ground beef, garlic powder and salt. Cook ground beef for 20 minutes at low heat. Do not brown. Set aside.

Heat chile sauce and set aside.

TO PREPARE ROLLED ENCHILADAS: Heat oil or shortening in frying pan. With tongs, quickly dip one tortilla at a time in hot oil and place it flat on a board or flat pan. Spoon about 2 tablespoons ground beef filling in center forming a line and sprinkle onions on filling. Roll tortilla with filling inside and place in shallow ungreased casserole dish. Place rolled enchilada with flap down. Repeat process until all tortillas are used, placing rolled enchiladas side by side in the baking dish.

Pour enough red chile sauce over enchiladas to moisten entire surface. Sprinkle with shredded cheese. Bake uncovered at 350° for 20 minutes. Remove from oven and garnish with shredded lettuce. Serve with sour cream topping. Enchiladas can be frozen. If stored in freezer, omit garnish and sour cream. (Serves 6)

ENCHILADAS ENROLLADAS CON ALMENDRAS
ROLLED ENCHILADAS WITH ALMONDS

12	corn tortillas
3 cups	cooked chicken or pork (shredded)
1 cup	green olives (chopped)
1	small size onion (chopped)
1 cup	almonds (slivered or chopped)
1 teaspoon	salt
1/4 teaspoon	garlic powder
1/4 teaspoon	black pepper (optional)
1/2 cup	cooking oil (for dipping tortillas)
1/2 cup	green onions (chopped)
1 1/2 cup	Cheddar cheese (shredded)
4 cups	Prepared Red Chile Sauce (heated)

Mix meat, olives, 1/2 cup almonds, onion, garlic powder and salt. Heat 2 tablespoons cooking oil in 2-quart saucepan and add the mixture. Simmer 5 minutes and set aside. Heat remaining oil in a separate skillet.

TO PREPARE ROLLED ENCHILADAS: follow the same preparation as recipe for Enchiladas De Rez Enrolladas substituting chicken almond filling. Sprinkle remaining cheese, almonds and green onions on top. Serve hot.

Will freeze without garnish. (Serves 6)

EMPANADAS FRITAS DE MASA FRESCA
FRIED TURNOVERS

2 cups	fresh masa
1/4 teaspoon	salt
2 tablespoons	water
1 1/2 cups	cheese (shredded) longhorn or Colby
1/2 cup	green chile (roasted, peeled and chopped; or canned chiles)
1 cup	shortening or cooking oil for deep frying

Mix masa with the water, salt and 1/2 cup shredded cheese. Mix well. Divide into 6 balls the size of a tennis ball. Flatten each ball between two pieces of waxed paper into a round patty about 5 or 6 inches in diameter. Remove top sheet of waxed paper. Fill the center with 1 tablespoon chopped green chiles and 2 tablespoons cheese. Fold over using the bottom sheet of waxed paper and seal the edges (press together). Place the turnover in preheated skillet with shortening Fry each side to a golden brown. remove and allow to drain on paper towel. Serve warm.

Uncooked turnovers can be frozen. (Yields 6)

EMPANADAS FRITAS DE MASA HARINA
FRIED TURNOVERS

1 cup	Masa Harina
1/4 teaspoon	salt
1 1/2 cup	cheese (shredded) Colby or longhorn
1/2 cup	green chiles (roasted, peeled and chopped)
3/4 cup	water
1 cup	shortening or cooking oil for deep frying

Mix Masa Harina with the salt, 1/2 cup shredded cheese and water. Divide into 6 balls the size of a tennis ball. Flatten each ball between 2 pieces of wax paper into a thin round patty about 5 or 6 inches in diameter. Remove top sheet. Fill the center with 1 tablespoon chopped green chile and 2 tablespoons cheese. Fold over using the bottom sheet of wax paper and seal the edges. Place the turnover in preheated skillet with shortening. Fry each side to a golden brown. Remove and allow to drain on paper towel.

Picadillo is also an excellent filling for empanadas. (see Picadillo recipe).

Uncooked turnovers can be frozen. (Yields 6)

PASTA DE CHILE COLORADO
RED CHILE PUREE

```
     12    red chile peppers (dry)
1 1/2 quarts  hot boiling water
  1 clove  garlic
```

Remove stems and seeds from peppers. wash in cold water, then soak in hot boiling water in covered pot for 20 minutes. remove the peppers, save the water and add during the grinding process.

Grind the peppers and garlic together creating a paste. Add small amounts of water until all water has been used. A blender is an excellent means to puree the chile.

For a fine puree paste, sieve the ground chile.

Store in refrigerator or freezer until ready to use. (Yields 1 1/2 quarts)

PASTA DE CHILE COLORADO-GUISADO
PREPARED RED CHILE SAUCE

```
    2 cups    red chile puree (basic recipe)
1/2 teaspoon  salt
1/2 teaspoon  garlic powder
2 tablespsons  lard or shortening
2 tablespoons  flour
```

Heat lard or shortening in a saucepan; add the flour, mix quickly and brown (similar to preparing gravy). Add chile puree and seasonings. Simmer 15 minutes, stirring intermittently.

NOTE: This Prepared Red Chile Sauce is a basic sauce used as an ingredient in various recipes in this book. Adding or decreasing the amount of flour will produce a thicker or thinner sauce, as desired. (Yields 2 cups)

CHILE CON CARNE-GUISADO
MEAT IN RED CHILE PUREE

2 pounds	lean beef (or pork) cut in small pieces
1/2 cup	shortening
1/2 cup	flour
5 cups	Red Chile Puree
1 1/2 teaspoons	salt
1/4 teaspoon	garlic powder
1 teaspoon	oregano

Heat the shortening in a saucepan. Dredge the meat in flour and brown in the shortening. Add remaining flour and mix thoroughly. Add the chile puree and seasoning. Cook slowly until the meat is tender, about 1 hour, or longer. (Serves 6)

CHILE COLORADO CON QUESO
RED CHILE SAUCE WITH CHEESE

2 cups	Prepared Red Chile Sauce
1/2 cup	chopped green onion
1/2 cup	shredded cheese (Colby or longhorn)

Mix ingredients in order; bring to a boil and simmer 5 minutes or until cheese has melted.

MOLE POBLANO
POBLANO SAUCE

SAUCE FOR MOLE POBLANO

6	chiles poblano
4	chiles ancho
4	chiles pasilla
1/3 cup	cooking oil
1/2 cup	drained cooked tomatoes
1/3 cups	oil

Slit chiles with knife, remove seeds, reserve 1 tbsp. seeds; heat oil and quickly fry chiles on both sides; set aside.

Place fried chiles in a 2 quart saucepan, cover with hot water and soak for 20 minutes.

In a food processor (with steel blade) or blender, puree soaked chiles and tomatoes. Heat one large skillet to medium hot, add oil, then add pureed chile and tomatoes. Cook 10 minutes, stirring constantly; set aside.

SPICES FOR MOLE POBLANO

Use frying skillet:

1/3 cup	oil
2 tablespoons	raisins
8	almonds, unskinned
2 oz.	pumpkin seeds hulled and toasted
	small stale corn tortilla (torn in pieces)
1 slice	stale bread
1 cup	water (use to form paste)

Heat oil in skillet. Fry raisins until puffy; remove with slotted spoon. In same skillet, fry almonds until brown, remove; fry pumpkin seeds briefly, remove. In same skillet,

MOLE POBLANO
POBLANO SAUCE CONTINUED

fry tortilla, remove; add bread and fry crisp. Blend all ingredients together, put in food processor using blade to puree and using some water to form paste.

    5 or 6 cups   of chicken broth
         4 oz.   semi-sweet chocolate

Add pureed mixture to the spices. Cook on medium flame for 5 minutes, stirring constantly, add chocolate pieces to the mixture. Cook 10 more minutes, stirring constantly. Add the broth and continue cooking for 30 more minutes, stirring constantly. Adjust seasonings. When oil floats up to the surface, mole is cooked. If it gets too thick, add a little more broth. Mole can be prepared one week in advance; it improves in flavor. It freezes well. This chile sauce can be used with cooked pork, turkey, chicken and stuffed chiles poblanos. (Yields approximately 1 1/2 pints)

CHILE CON CARNE PARA TAMALES
CHILE CON CARNE FOR TAMALES

4 pounds	meat (boneless chuck roast, pork roast, or half and half)
2 1/2 quarts	water
1 1/2 teaspoons	salt
1 clove	garlic
6 cups	Prepared Red Chile Sauce (see basic recipe) for a thicker sauce add 3 tablespoons flour
2	tablespoons shortening

Place the meat and water in a large kettle, add salt and garlic. Cover kettle, heat and bring to a boil. Cook at low heat for 3 or 3 1/2 hours until meat is tender. Remove meat from broth and allow to cool. Cut meat into bite size pieces and set aside.

Heat shortening in a large saucepan. Add flour and brown lightly. Add the Prepared Chile Sauce and bring to a boil, simmer for 5 minutes stirring the sauce intermittently.

Add the meat to the chile sauce and simmer 10 to 15 minutes stirring occasionally. Allow to cool. Refrigerate until ready to use. Will store in freezer. (Yields 2 quarts for approx. 4 dozen tamales)

TAMALES DE CHILE CON CARNE DE MASA FRESCA
RED CHILE BEEF TAMALES

2 quarts	Prepared Chile Con Carne (use basic recipe)
5 pounds	fresh masa
1 1/2 pounds	lard
1 tablespoon	salt
2 - 3 cups	cold tap water
1 1/2 pounds	corn husks

TO PREPARE THE MASA: Whip the lard and salt until fluffy (about 2 minutes). Add masa gradually, alternating with water, until all the masa and approximately 2 cups of water are used. Beat until fluffy and test by placing small sample into a glass of water. If sample rises, masa is ready. If masa is too dry, add enough water to bring masa to a spreading consistency. Set aside.

NOTE: Use an electric mixer to whip.

TO PREPARE CORN HUSKS: Soak in hot water for about 10 minutes until husks are flexible. Wash and drain. Select the large husks for making tamales.

TO MAKE TAMALES: Spread approximately 1 heaping tablespoon of masa on the broad end of the corn husk (side to side and half way up). Place 2 heaping tablespoons of chile con carne ln center and roll sides of husk together so that edges overlap. Bend the narrow end toward tamale and pinch open (opposite) edge together.

TO COOK TAMALES: To cook 2 dozen tamales, use a large pot. Crumple a piece of tinfoil to the size of a cup and place it in center of the pot. Add 2 cups of water and carefully place the tamales around the tinfoil (open end up) making sure the flap is against the foil and in pyramid fashion, until all the tamales have been assembled in the pot. Cover tightly and steam cook for about 40 minutes.

Continued on next page

RED CHILE BEEF TAMALES CONTINUED

NOTE: Uncooked tamales will store in freezer. To cook, do not thaw, simply double the steam cooking time. (Yields 4 1/2 dozen)

TAMALES DE CHILE CON CARNE DE MASA HARINA
RED CHILE BEEF TAMALES

5 cups	Masa Harina
2 cups	shortening
2 teaspoons	salt
4 1/3 cups	meat broth (COOL)
1 pound	corn husks
2 quarts	Prepared Chile Con Carne

TO PREPARE CORN HUSKS: Follow same procedure as recipe Tamales De Chile Con Carne De Masa Fresca.

Whip the lard and salt with electric mixer until fluffy. Add Masa Harina, salt and broth, and beat until light and fluffy Test marble-size sample in cup of cold water; masa will float when "ready."

TO MAKE AND COOK TAMALES: Follow same procedure as recipe for Tamales De Chile Con Carne De Masa Fresca. (Yields 4 dozen)

PASTEL DE CHILE CON CARNE DE MASA FRESCA
TAMALE PIE

4 cups	masa fresca
1/4 cup	water
1 teaspoon	salt
2/3 cup	shortening
4 cups	Prepared Chile Con Carne (use basic recipe)
1/2 cup	green olives (sliced)

Place shortening in a bowl and beat until fluffy. Add masa, salt and water. Beat mixture until fluffy and test it by placing a spoonful of masa in cup of cold water. Masa is "ready" when sample floats in water. If needed, gradually add more water to reach spreading consistency.

TO MAKE TAMALE PIES: Divide masa into 4 equal portions. Grease 9 inch pie plates. Spread 1/4 masa to form pie shell. Place 2 cups Chile Con Carne in pie shell and spread evenly. Sprinkle 1/4 cup green olives over Chile Con Carne. Spread 1/4 masa over Chile Con Carne to form top crust. Repeat same procedure for second pie.

Uncooked tamale pies can be stored in freezer until ready to use.

TO BAKE: Bake pies 30 minutes in preheated oven at 400° for a golden brown crust.

To bake frozen pie, do not thaw, simply bake longer, or until crust is golden brown. (Yields 2 pies)

PASTEL DE CHILE CON CARNE MASA HARINA
TAMALE PIE

3 cups	Masa Harina
3 1/4 cups	water
1 teaspoon	salt
1 cup	shortening
4 cups	Prepared Chile Con Carne (see basic recipe)
1/2 cup	green olives (pitted)

Place shortening in a bowl and beat until fluffy. Add Masa Harina, salt and water. Beat mixture until fluffy. Test by placing a spoonful of masa in cup of cold water. Masa is "ready" when sample floats in the water.

TO PREPARE AND BAKE: Follow instructions as for recipe for Pastel De Chile Con Carne De Masa Fresca. (Yields 2 pies)

TAMALES DE ELOTE
GREEN CORN TAMALES

4 dozen	white sweet corn (fresh - medium hard kernel)
1	small zucchini (chopped)
3 1/2 cups	shortening
2 tablespoons	salt
1 pound	Colby or longhorn yellow cheese (grated or cut in 2" strips)
1 1/2 cups	green chile peppers (equivalent to one 10 oz. can, chopped or prepared in long slivered strips) Amount of green chile peppers used varies according to personal taste.

Continued on next page

TAMALES DE ELOTE
GREEN CORN TAMALES CONTINUED

TO REMOVE HUSKS: Take the fresh corn, remove and save husks. To remove the husks, cut 2 or 3 inches from the top (enough to barely cut off the tip of the cob and the corn silk) and cut enough from the base of the corn to reach the kernel area. This facilitates removal of the husks without damaging the husks or losing the kernels. Wash husks, drain and set aside for later use.

TO PREPARE MASA: Clean the cob, blade the corn kernels with an electric knife and grind together with squash in a food chopper (medium coarse). This yields about 6 quarts.

Use electric beater to whip shortening with salt until fluffy. Combine shortening mixture and ground corn to form masa. Mix thoroughly with spoon.

The grated cheese and chopped chiles may be mixed into the masa or chile and cheese strips may be added after the batter (masa) is spooned onto the husk to make the tamale. Place strip of cheese and strip of green chile in center of masa.

TO MAKE THE TAMALES: The corn mixture (masa) should be thick. Select the biggest husks for the tamales. Take one husk, place 3 tablespoonsful of the masa in the center, fold edges toward center and overlap, then bring pointed end of husk down and turn the tamale over to keep it intact. Repeat this procedure until all the masa is used up.

TO COOK THE TAMALES: Follow same directions as for Tamales De Chile Con Carne De Masa Fresca. (Yields 6 dozen tamales, 1 dozen serves 4 or 6)

NOTE: This sauce is to be used hot. Use as topping on individual servings of cooked or canned whole beans. Makes excellent fondue.

PASTEL DE ELOTE
GREEN CORN TAMALE PIE

6	ears fresh white corn
1/2 cup	chopped zucchini + 1 cup water
1/2 cup	shortening
1	egg
1/2 teaspoon	salt
1/2 teaspoon	black pepper
1 1/2 teaspoon	baking powder
1 cup	shredded cheese (Colby or Cheddar)
4	green chile peppers (roasted peeled and chopped or canned)

TO REMOVE THE HUSKS: Follow the same instructions as for recipe Tamales De Elote

TO PREPARE MASA: Clean the cob, blade the corn kernels with a sharp knife or electric knife. Combine kernels and chopped squash. Use blender to make a coarsely ground mixture, blending 1 1/2 cup at a time with a little water, until all the corn squash mixture has been ground and all the water has been used. Whip shortening until fluffy, add egg and whip again. Combine with the ground corn mixture, seasonings, baking powder, cheese and chopped green chiles. Mix well.

TO MAKE PIES: Grease 2 8-inch pie plates and pour mixture. bake in a preheated oven at 375° for 40 minutes. Uncooked pies can be frozen.

TAMALES DE FRIJOL DE MASA FRESCA
BEAN TAMALES

FILLING:

4 cups	cooked beans (drain liquid, mash)
4 tablespoons	lard
1 cup	crushed panocha or dark brown sugar
1 teaspoon	cinnamon
1 teaspoon	cloves
2 cups	seedless raisins (soak in hot water for 1/2 hour)

Heat lard in skillet. Combine beans, brown sugar, spices and raisins. Simmer mixture for 15 minutes, stirring frequently to prevent beans from burning. Set aside to cool.

MASA FOR TAMALES:

2/3 cup	lard (measure and whip)
1 1/2 pound	fresh masa
1 1/2 teaspoons	salt
2 tablespoons	sugar
1 cup	water

TO PREPARE AND COOK: Follow same directions as for Tamales De Chile Con Carne. (Yields 2 dozen)

TAMALES DE FRIJOL DE MASA HARINA
BEAN TAMALES

Use the same amount of bean filling as recipe for Tamales De Masa Fresca.

MASA HARINA (MASA HARINA DOUGH)

1 cup	lard
2 1/2 cups	Masa Harina
1 teaspoon	salt
3 tablespoons	sugar
1 3/4 cups	water

Follow the same procedure to make and cook as recipe for Tamales De Chile Con Carne.
Uncooked tamales can be frozen. (Yields 2 dozen)

FRIJOLES PINTOS
PINTO BEANS, BASIC RECIPE

2 cups	pinto beans
1 teaspoon	salt
6 cups	hot water
8 tablespoons	bacon drippings

Clean the beans (remove dirt, stones and foreign matter). Rinse in cold water. Place beans in cooking pot, add 6 cups hot water. Soak for 2 hours, then add salt.

Heat water to boiling and cook beans over low flame for 3 1/2 hours or until tender. If more water is added, it should be boiling hot.

Add bacon drippings 1 hour before beans are done. Beans are ready to eat. Cooked beans can be frozen. (Serves 8)

FRIJOLES FRITOS
FRIED BEANS

4 cups	cooked beans (basic recipe)
1/2 cup	lard or shortening
1/2 cup	cheese, shredded (Colby or longhorn)

Heat lard in a skillet. Add the beans and some liquid and mash beans, stirring bean mixture until it thickens. Simmer 10 minutes, stirring the beans constantly, as they burn easily, then add cheese. Stir once or twice until cheese is melted.

Fried beans can be frozen. (Serves 6)

FRIJOLES REFRITOS
REFRIED BEANS

4 cups	fried beans
1/3 cup	lard
1/3 cup	shredded cheese (jack or Colby)

Heat lard in a skillet. Add fried beans and cheese. Simmer 10 to 15 minutes stirring frequently. This bean dish will be thicker than the fried beans. Refried beans can be frozen. (Serves 6)

FRIJOLES REFRITOS AL HORNO
REFRIED BEANS - BAKED

4 cups	refried pinto beans (see previous recipe)
1/4 cup	water
1/2 cup	Cheddar or Colby cheese (shredded)

Thoroughly mix refried beans and water. Simmer for 10 minutes. Place in deep casserole dish and bake in oven at low temperature, about 250°, for 20 minutes. Remove from oven and sprinkle cheese over the beans while still hot.

Choose any of the hot sauces to garnish the beans.

COPYRIGHT AMALIA RUIZ CLARK, 1986

FRIJOLES CON CARNE
BEANS WITH MEAT

2 cups	beans (uncooked)
1 pound	short ribs (beef or pork cut into 2" pieces)
8 cups	hot water
1 teaspoon	salt
1/8 teaspoon	garlic powder

Clean beans (remove dirt, stones and foreign matter) and rinse in cold water. Place beans in cooking pot and add the hot water. Soak for 2 hours. Add short ribs and seasonings to beans. Heat water to boiling and cook over low flame for 3 1/2 hours or until tender. May be stored in freezer. (Serves 8)

FRIJOLES CON CHILE
MEXICAN CHILE BEANS

2 cups	cooked whole pinto beans
1 cup	chorizo (refer to recipe for chorizo)
1 cup	red chile puree
	salt to taste
1 tablespoon	shortening

Heat shortening in a skillet, add chorizo and cook, but do not brown. Drain excess fat.

Place beans in cooking pot, add cooked chorizo and the red chile puree. Allow to simmer at low heat for 35 minutes and add liquid from beans to desired thickness. Salt to taste. (Serves 6)

COPYRIGHT AMALIA RUIZ CLARK, 1986

FRIJOLES FRITOS CON CHILES
BEANS WITH RED CHILE PEPPERS

    2 cups   cooked, mashed beans (with bean liquid)
    1/2 cup   lard or shortening
    2   dried red chile peppers

Wash, scoop seeds out, and break red chile peppers into medium size pieces. Heat lard in skillet, fry the red chiles until golden brown, and add beans. Stir and simmer for 15 to 20 minutes.

It may be served as a side dish with flour or corn tortillas. (Serves 6)

POSOLE
BEANS, HOMINY AND PORK HOCKS

    2 cups   cooked beans (whole)
    2 cups   hominy (drained), or one 16-oz. can
    2 large   fresh pork hocks (split in 2 or 3 pieces)
    2 quarts   water
    2 teaspoons   salt
    1   clove garlic

Place the pork hocks in a large kettle with the water, salt and garlic. Cook for 2 1/2 or 3 hours. Remove hocks. Allow hocks and broth to cool. Remove meat from hocks, cut meat into small pieces. Skim off the fat from the cooled broth; save 3 cups of broth. Add meat, beans and hominy to broth and simmer for 20 minutes.

Hot seasoning, such as hot peppers, fresh or pickled, can be used on individual servings for zest. (Serves 6 to 8)

Copyright Amalia Ruiz Clark, 1986

TORTILLAS DE HARINA
FLOUR TORTILLAS

8 cups	all purpose flour
1½ tablespoons	salt
1/2 cup	lard or shortening
3 1/4 cups	warm water

Mix dry ingredients in a large bowl. Using hands, blend lard into flour mixture. Gradually add warm water to the mixture until a soft textured dough (not sticky) is obtained.

Knead dough for 10 minutes, pat lightly with lard, cover and let stand 15 minutes.

Repeat above instructions. Dough should be smooth.

Divide dough into 24 balls slightly bigger than a tennis ball. Pat each ball with lard, cover with wax paper and let stand for 30 minutes.

Traditionally, the flour tortilla can be patted and shaped by hand; however, a rolling pin can be used. Use floured board to roll the balls into very thin rounds. (Approximately 16 inches in diameter).

Use a large heated iron griddle (ungreased) for cooking. Lay the rolledout tortilla on the griddle and cook momentarily (dough will bubble a little); then lift, flip and cook the other side. Tortillas will be browned in the areas where the dough bubbled and some areas will remain white, but will be cooked.

Cooked tortillas can be frozen and used as needed. Tortillas may be used with meals in the same fashion bread is used. (Yields 24)

TORTILLAS DE HARINA DE ESPAURA
FLOUR TORTILLAS WITH BAKING POWDER

8 cups	all purpose flour
1½ tablespoon	salt
2 tablespoons	baking powder
2/3 cup	lard or shortening
3 to 3 1/3 cups	water or milk (warm)

TO MAKE TORTILLAS: Follow the same instructions as recipe for Tortillas De Harina, except divide dough into 36 balls the size of a golf ball.

These tortillas will be smaller and slightly thicker.

SOPAPILLAS
BREAD PUFFS

2 cups	flour
2 teaspoons.	baking powder
1 teaspoon	salt
1 tablespoon	sugar
3 tablespoons	shortening
2/3 cup	warm water
1 1/2 cups	cooking oil (for deep frying)

Mix dry ingredients. Add shortening and cut in coarsely. Add water gradually, kneading dough for about 5 to 8 minutes. Cover and allow to stand for 15 minutes.

Roll dough into a thin rectangular sheet about 1/8 inch thick. Cut into 3-inch squares. Deep fry in hot oil until puffy and bread turns a golden brown. Drain on paper towel. Delicious with meals, plain or with honey. (Yields 2 1/2 dozen)

SOPAS

(Soups)

Copyright Amalia Ruiz Clark, 1986

SOPA DE ALBONDIGAS
MEXICAN MEAT BALL SOUP

1 pound	ground beef
1	egg
1/2 teaspoon	salt
1/2 teaspoon	black pepper
1/8 teaspoon	garlic powder
2 teaspoons	ground cilantro seeds
1/4 cup	fresh cilantro (minced)
2	green onions (chopped)
1	green chile - optional (roasted, peeled and chopped or canned)
1	fresh tomato (chopped)
1/2 cup	Bisquick flour
1 quart	water (add 1/2 teaspoon salt, or to taste)

Mix all ingredients except water. Form meat balls about the size of a walnut.

In a 2-quart saucepan, bring salted water to a hard boil. Add meat balls to boiling water and cook 30 minutes over low flame in covered pot.

This soup can be prepared in advance and stored in refrigerator until ready to use. Can also be stored in freezer. (Serves 4)

SOPA DE LENTEJAS
LENTIL SOUP

1 pound	lentils
2 quarts	water
2 teaspoons	salt
1/4 cup	fresh green onions (finely chopped)
1/4 cup	fresh cilantro (Coursely chopped)
1/3 cup	shortening

Wash lentils and place in a large kettle. Add 2 quarts water and salt. Cover kettle and bring water to a boil. Reduce heat and simmer 45 minutes.

In a skillet, sauté onions and cilantro in 1/3 cup shortening, but do not brown. Add this to the lentils. Cover and simmer 25 minutes. Serve hot. This soup can be stored in freezer.

SOPA DE FRIJOLES NEGRO CON LENTEJAS
BLACK BEAN AND LENTIL SOUP

1-1/2 cup	black beans
1/2 cup	brown lentils
1/2 cup	pureed tomatoes
1	garlic clove (minced)
1	small onion (chopped)
1	pickled jalapeño chile (minced)
5 to 6 cups	chicken broth or chicken bouillon
	Sprigs of fresh cilantro and green onions

Clean and wash beans. Soak beans in hot water for 2 hours. Drain beans and place in a kettle. Add broth and cook for 2 hours. Clean and wash lentils; add to the beans. Add the tomatoes, garlic, onion, and jalapeño. Simmer for 45 to 50 minutes. Adjust seasonings to taste. Garnish with sprigs of fresh cilantro and chopped green onions. Serves 8.

Note: Serve with sopapillas or corn chips.

Copyright Amalia Ruiz Clark, 1986

SOPA DE FIDEO
VERMICELLI SOUP

1 pound	fideo (vermicelli)
1/2 cup	shortening
1/2 cup	tomato sauce
1 teaspoon	salt, or to taste
1 dash	garlic powder
2	green onions (chopped)
5 cups	chicken or beef broth (hot)

In a wide skillet fry fideo coils in shortening, turning coils until golden brown on both sides. Transfer the browned fideo coils to a saucepan, add broth and remaining ingredients. Cover and simmer over low flame for 20 minutes. Stir once or twice separating coils with a long fork. Continue cooking in uncovered saucepan until no longer watery. Soup may be prepared in advance. Flavor improves with reheating.

Can be used as a side dish with main meat dishes. (Serves 8)

Copyright Amalia Ruiz Clark, 1986

SOPA DE POLLO
CHICKEN SOUP

1	fryer and gizzards
2 quarts	water
1 teaspoon	salt
1/4 teaspoon	garlic
1/2 cup	rice
1 tablespoon	oil
7 cups	chicken broth
1	fresh tomato (chopped)
1	medium onion (chopped)
3	celery stalks (cut in 1-inch pieces)

Disjoint fryer and place in large pot. Add water and seasoning. Bring to a boil and skim top foam. Cover and simmer 45 minutes. Remove chicken from broth and allow chicken to cool. Save broth. Debone chicken. Cube chicken and gizzards.

Heat oil in saucepan and brown the rice lightly. Add tomato and onions to rice and mix. Add chicken broth and celery. Cover and simmer 25 minutes. Add. the cubed chicken and gizzards. Simmer 15 minutes. Serve hot. May be stored in refrigerator or freezer. (Serves 8)

Copyright Amalia Ruiz Clark, 1986

CALDO DE QUESO
CHEESE SOUP

2 tablespoons	extra virgin olive oil
1 medium	onion, chopped
3	garlic cloves, minced
1 medium	potato, peeled and cubed
1/4 cup	green chiles, roasted and peeled or canned
1 quart	hot chicken or beef broth
1 cup	mozzarella cheese grated
	Salt and freshly ground pepper
	Fresh cilantro
4	limes

Heat oil in skillet over medium heat. Saute onion, garlic, potato and chiles, for 3 minutes. Place in a pot with hot broth, bring to a boil. Lower heat and simmer for 25 minutes. Add 1/2 of the cheese and simmer until cheese melts. Serve in soup bowls. Garnish with a sprig of cilantro. Sprinkle some cheese and add 2 slices of lime. Have corn chips or hard rolls with soup. (Serves 6)

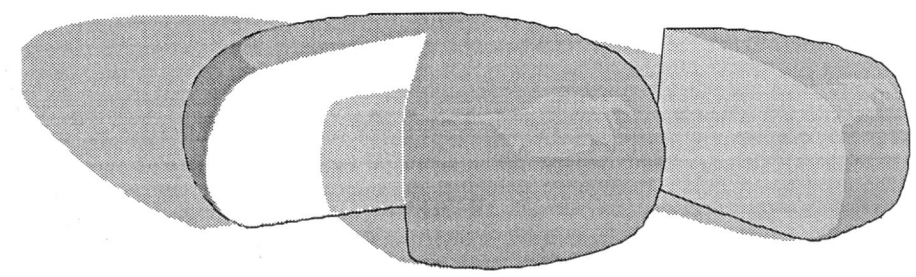

COPYRIGHT AMALIA RUIZ CLARK, 1986

CASUELA DE CARNE SECA MACHACADA
SHREDDED JERKY SOUP

2 cups	shredded jerky
2 1/2 tablespoons	shortening
2 tablespoons	flour
1/2 cup	chopped onion
1/2 cup	canned tomatoes
1/3 cup	green chile peppers (roasted, peeled and chopped or canned)
1/2 teaspoon	salt
dash	of black pepper
2 1/2 cups	water

Heat shortening in saucepan. Add flour and brown lightly. Add onion, tomatoes, green chile and salt. Mix ingredients well. Add shredded jerky turning and mixing briskly. Add 2 1/2 cups water. Simmer 15 minutes. Serve hot. (Serves 4)

PUCHERO
MEXICAN STEW

3 pounds	short ribs (lean beef)
1	large onion
4	cloves garlic
2 teaspoons	salt
3	ears of fresh corn (cut into 2-inch pieces)
4	medium white potatoes (cut in half)
4	large carrots (cut each into 3 pieces)
1 pound	fresh green string beans (whole)
1 15-oz. can	garbanzo beans
4	medium zucchini squash (cut in half) (Optional) Variety of squash cut in medium pieces
1	medium head white cabbage (cut into quarters)
1 8-oz. can	tomato sauce

Place short ribs in a large pot. Fill with enough water to cover the meat. Add salt, garlic cloves and onion. Bring to a full boil. Skim foam until broth no longer foams. Cover and boil at medium or low heat for 3 hours, or until meat is tender. Remove onion and garlic cloves. Add vegetables in the order listed (layered) without mixing. Pour tomato sauce crisscrossed over layered vegetables. Simmer 1/2 hour.

COPYRIGHT AMALIA RUIZ CLARK, 1986

MENUDO
TRIPE SOUP

5 pounds	tripe (for menudo)
2	calves feet (optional)
1 pound	nixtamal corn, or 2 28-oz. cans of hominy
2 tablespoons	salt
6 or 7 quarts	of water

Wash tripe well and cut into 2-inch squares, or bite size pieces. Wash calves feet, put in a large pot. Cover with water and cook at low heat for 1 1/2 hours. Add tripe, corn, salt and garlic. Simmer 6 hours more, until tender and firm but not mushy.

If canned hominy is used, add last after menudo has cooked for 5 hours.

If calves feet are not used, simmer tripe for 6 hours.

Serve hot, garnish with fresh minced onions and fresh coriander, crushed chile tepíns or hot chile sauce for zest. Menudo stores well in freezer. Menudo soup is a New Year's Eve favorite. (serves 20 to 24)

SOPA DE TORTILLA
TORTILLA SOUP

10	corn tortillas, stale, if fresh let dry for frying
1/3 cup	olive oil
1	onion, chopped
6	garlic cloves, minced
1/2 cup	green chiles, roasted, peeled and chopped or canned
1/2 cup	Mexican cheese, or cheese of choice, grated
1 quart	hot chicken or beef broth
	Salt and freshly ground pepper to taste
	Garnish with lime slices, sour cream and avocados

Cut tortillas into 1/4 inch strips; fry until crisp, remove from skillet and drain on paper towel. In same skillet sauté onion, garlic and chiles. In a 2 quart sauce pan place onion, garlic, chiles, 1/2 of the tortillas and pour in hot broth. Bring to a boil, lower heat and simmer for 25 minutes. Adjust seasonings. Garnish with more corn chips, cilantro, lime slices, sour cream and avocado slices.

Variation: for a red tortilla soup omit green chiles - sauté 1 cup tomatoe puree and 1 cup chile puree in 1 teaspoon olive oil for 3 minutes and add to broth. See recipe for chile puree.

COPYRIGHT AMALIA RUIZ CLARK, 1986

ENSALADAS

SALADS

ENSALADA DE ARANDANO
CRANBERRY SALAD MOLD

1 pound	fresh cranberries (use 1 cup cooked)
2 cups	water
1 1/2 cups	sugar
1 6-oz. package	cherry or raspberry gelatin
1 tablespoon	lemon juice
1 cup	chopped walnuts
1/2 pint	whipping cream (2 cups whipped)

Place 2 cups water and sugar in saucepan and boil. Add cranberries after sugar dissolves, cook 10 minutes or until berry skins pop. Remove from heat and let cool.

Make gelatin as directed on package, decreasing amount of water called for by 1 cup. Add 1 cup cranberries, lemon juice and walnuts to gelatin. Place in refrigerator. When gelatin starts to thicken, fold in 2 cups whipped cream. Pour into a mold and chill until firm. (Serves 10)

ENSALADA DE FRUTA FRESCA
FRESH FRUIT SALAD

1	fresh pineapple (cored and cubed)
2	oranges (peeled and cut into small pieces)
2	bananas (cut into 1-inch pieces)
16	cantaloupe melon balls
16	watermelon balls
20	seedless grapes
4 tablespoons	lime juice or lemon juice
6 ounces	Kirschwasser Cherry Brandy

Combine fruits, juice and brandy. Mix thoroughly. Chill at least 6 hours.

SERVING SUGGESTION: Serve with Pollo Asado Con Arroz or Guajolote Asado Con Relleno A La Mexicana. (Serves 10 to 12)

ENSALADA DE PAPAYA Y CIRUELA
PAPAYA PLUM SALAD

3	papayas
12	red plums
12	purple grapes
12	red grapes

Cut papaya in half, scoop seeds out and arrange papaya halves on lettuce leaves. Fill papaya halves with red and purple grapes. Place red plums (cut in half and pitted) alongside papayas.

Garnish with Adorno De Crema Agria Para Ensalada recipe on the following page. (Serves 6)

ADORNO DE CREMA AGRIA PARA ENSALADA
SOUR CREAM DRESSING

- 1 cup   dairy sour cream
- 1/2 cup   Miracle Whip Salad Dressing
- 1/2 cup   canned crushed pineapple with heavy syrup

Combine all the ingredients in a mixing bowl and mix thoroughly. Pour into a bowl, cover and chill. (Yields 2 cups)

ENSALADA DE AGUACATE
AVOCADO SALAD

- 2   ripe avocados
- 2   fresh tomatoes (small)
- 4   celery heart sticks
- 8   radishes
- 1/2   head lettuce
- 1/2 teaspoon   salt
- dash   of black pepper

Peel and pit avocados. Cut into bite-size pieces. Cut tomatoes into small wedges. Cut celery heart sticks into 1/2 inch strips. Cut radishes in half. Cube lettuce. Toss ingredients together. Add salt and dash of black pepper. Refrigerate before serving. Garnish with Adorno De Vinagre Para Ensalada (see Salad Dressing recipe).

COPYRIGHT AMALIA RUIZ CLARK, 1986

ENSALADA DE NOPALITOS
NOPALITOS SALAD

2 cups	nopalitos, cooked and drained (basic recipe or canned)
1/2	onion (sliced into very thin onion rings)
1 cup	baby beets - drained and cut in quarters
2 eggs,	hard boiled (for garnish)

Mix ingredients in order, except the eggs. Cut eggs into rings approximately 1/4 inch thick. Garnish salad with egg rings. Garnish with Adorno De Vinagre Para Ensalada. (Serves 6)

ADORNO DE VINAGRE PARA ENSALADA
VINEGAR SALAD DRESSING

1/2 cup	white wine vinegar
1/2 cup	extra virgin olive oil
2 tablespoons	sugar
1 teaspoon	salt
1 teaspoon	freshly ground pepper
1 clove	of garlic, minced

Mix with wisk and pour into glass container, cover with lid. Store in refrigerator until ready to use. (Yields 8 onces)

ENSALADA DE CAMARÓN
SHRIMP SALAD

2 cups	small shrimp (cooked and drained or canned)
1	bell pepper (minced)
1/2	head lettuce (tear in small
10	cherry tomatoes
2	celery stalks (cut in 1-inch pieces)
1	small cucumber (peel and slice)
1/2 cup	radishes (minced)
2	green onions and tops (minced)
1/2 teaspoon	salt
1/4 teaspoon	black pepper
4 tablespoons	mayonnaise
2	hard boiled eggs
1	teaspoon paprika

Combine all ingredients in large bowl (except eggs and paprika), toss lightly.

Garnish salad with sliced eggs and sprinkle with paprika. (Serves 8)

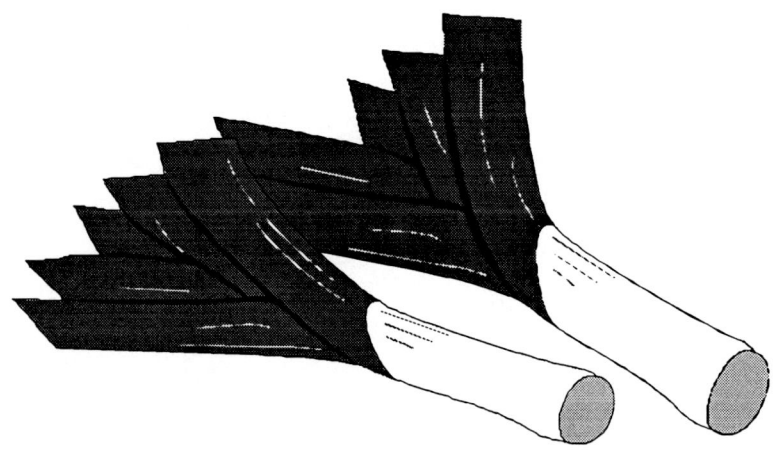

Copyright Amalia Ruiz Clark, 1986

ENSALADA DE PAPA
POTATO SALAD

4	medium potatoes (diced)
1	medium dill or sour pickle (finely diced)
2	sweet midget pickles (finely diced)
2	green onions and stems (chopped)
2	medium celery sticks (finely diced)
1	small delicious red apple (minced)
2	large radishes (finely diced)
6	hard boiled eggs (minced)
1 teaspoon	salt
1/4 teaspoon	coarse black pepper
12 ounces	Best Food Mayonnaise
2 tablespoons	tartar sauce
8	pitted ripe olives (diced)

Mix ingredients in order, except diced olives. Mix the salad lightly. Add diced olives and mix lightly. Garnish and refrigerate.

GARNISH FOR ENSALADA DE PAPA

1/2	delicious apple (sliced)
2	radishes

Garnish potato salad with apple and radish slices. Top with one whole radish in center surrounded by 6 olives. Refrigerate salad at least 2 hours before serving.

ENSALADA DE SALPICON
BEEF TONGUE SALAD

1	beef tongue
2	medium sized potatoes
1 16-oz. can	seasoned green beans French style
1	small onion
1	fresh tomato
6	crisp lettuce leaves (romaine)
1/4 cup	vinegar
2 tablespoons	vegetable oil
1 tablespoon	water
1 teaspoon	salt
1/4 teaspoon	black pepper

Cook beef tongue 2 1/2 to 3 hours until tender. Let cool. Remove skin and cut into thin slices.

Cook potatoes. Let cool and slice medium thin. Set aside. Slice onion into thin rings. Drain green beans.

Mix vinegar, oil, water, salt and pepper. Pour 1/2 mixture over drained green beans; use other half on onion rings. Marinate separately for 1/2 hour. Drain and save marinade.

Arrange prepared ingredients in layers on large serving platter. Place lettuce leaves around serving platter, followed by layer of sliced potatoes, layer of green beans, and layer of onion rings. Then top with layer of sliced beef tongue and garnish with tomato slices. Pour remaining marinade to moisten salpicon. (Serves 8)

ENSALADA DE NOCHE BUENA
CHRISTMAS EVE SALAD

4	beets, cooked and sliced
1 cup	pineapple cubes, fresh or canned
2	red apples, unpeeled and sliced
2	bananas, sliced
2	oranges, peeled and sliced
1/3 cup	roasted peanuts
1/3 cup	pine nuts
1/4 cup	pomegranate seeds
1/2 cup	Rice vinegar for dressing
	Romaine lettuce for garnish

Place lettuce on a salad platter. Arrange slices of fruit in an alternating pattern on top of lettuce. Sprinkle nuts and pomegranate seeds on fruit. Sprinkle rice vinegar over salad. (Serves 10)

COMIDAS CON HUEVOS

(EGG DISHES)

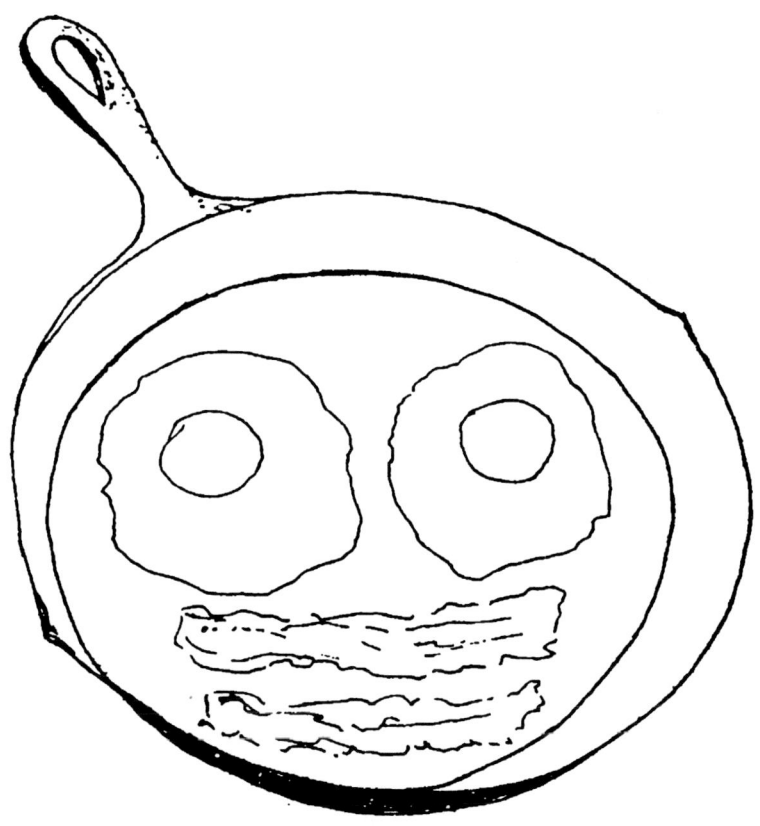

HUEVOS RANCHEROS
RANCH STYLE EGGS

4	eggs
2 tablespoons	butter
	salt (to taste)
4	tortillas, flour or corn
1/2 cup	shortening or cooking oil
1 pint	Salsa Picante De Tomate Con Cebolla (see recipe)
1/4 cup	Colby or Cheddar Cheese (shredded)

Melt 2 tablespoons butter in 10 or 12 inch skillet over medium to low heat. Fry or poach eggs. Heat hot salsa. Place fried tortillas on individual dishes and spoon hot salsa evenly on tortilla. Top with one or two fried or poached eggs. Spoon salsa over eggs and garnish with cheese.

Prepare tortillas before hand. Fry in a separate skillet at medium heat, one at a time, until slightly crisp. Drain on paper towel. (Serves 2 or 4)

HUEVOS A LA BENEDICT
EN TORTITAS DE MASA
EGGS BENEDICT ON MASA PATTIES

6	eggs
6	fried patties (masa fresca or Masa Harina)

See recipe for Enchiladas Chatas. Use masa fresca or Masa Harina to make patties. Poach or fry the egg and place on the patty. Garnish with a hot sauce. (Serves 4)

HUEVOS REVUELTOS CON CARNE SECA MACHACADA
EGGS SCRAMBLED WITH SHREDDED JERKY

1 cup	shredded jerky
4	eggs
5 tablespoons	shortening
4	green onions (chopped)
1/2 teaspoon	salt
1/4 teaspoon	pepper

Heat shortening in skillet, add onions and sauté. Add jerky, mix thoroughly. Add eggs, salt and pepper and scramble the mixture until well cooked.

This dish is excellent for brunch. Tasty when topped with any of the hot sauces. (Serves 4)

HUEVOS REVUELTOS CON NOPALITOS
SCRAMBLED EGGS WITH PRICKLY PEAR CACTUS

1/2 cup	nopalitos (cooked and drained or canned)
3	thin slices onion
2 tablespoons	butter or shortening
4	eggs
1 tablespoon	milk
1/4 teaspoon	salt
1/4 teaspoon	black pepper
1/4 cup	shredded cheese (Cheddar or Colby)

Heat butter in a skillet. Sauté onion slices, add nopalitos and heat well. Beat eggs with seasonings and pour over nopalitos and scramble.

Garnish with shredded cheese and top with any of the hot sauces. Serve with hot flour or corn tortillas. (Serves 4)

COPYRIGHT AMALIA RUIZ CLARK, 1986

HUEVOS REVUELTOS CON CHORIZO
SCRAMBLED EGGS WITH HOT SAUSAGE

1 cup	chorizo (Mexican hot sausage)
2 tablespoons	shortening
4	eggs
	salt (to taste)

Heat shortening in skillet. Add chorizo and fry until done, separating the sausage with a fork as it cooks. Beat eggs; add to the chorizo. Stir with a fork as you would scrambled eggs. (Serves 4)

HUEVOS REVUELTOS CON PAPAS
SCRAMBLED EGGS WITH POTATOES

2	medium potatoes (cubed)
1/3 cup	shortening & 2 tablespoons bacon drippings
1/2 teaspoon	black pepper
1	medium onion (chopped)
1	bell pepper (chopped)
6	eggs
1/2 teaspoon	salt
6	bacon strips, fried crisp and crumbled

Heat shortening in a skillet. Add potatoes and seasonings. Cover skillet and cook over low heat for 15 to 20 minutes. Turn frequently, do not brown. Add onions and bell pepper. Mix together and cook for 5 minutes. Add beaten eggs with salt and crumbled bacon. Mix thoroughly until well done. Use any of the hot sauces for a zesty flavor. Serve with flour tortillas. (Serves 8)

COPYRIGHT AMALIA RUIZ CLARK, 1986

HUEVOS REVUELTOS CON TORTILLAS TOSTADAS
SCRAMBLED EGGS WITH TORTILLA CHIPS

4	eggs (beaten)
	tortillas (cut into bite size pieces)
3 tablespoons	shortening
1/4 cup	chopped green onions
1 or 2	crumbled chile tepins (optional)
4 tablespoons	grated longhorn or Cheddar cheese
	salt and pepper (to taste)

Fry tortilla pieces until crisp. Add onion, eggs and seasoning (chile tepins optional). Stir as you would for scrambled eggs and cook until done. Sprinkle with cheese and serve.

Good for brunch or breakfast.

TORTILLA DE HUEVOS CON CHILE VERDE
GREEN CHILE OMELET

4	eggs
4 tablespoons	cream or milk
1/4 teaspoon	salt
1/4 teaspoon	black pepper
2 tablespoons	butter or shortening
1/2 cup	green chiles (roasted, peeled, and chopped or canned)
1/2 cup	Cheddar cheese (shredded)

Heat butter or shortening in a skillet. Beat eggs together with cream or milk and seasonings. Cook omelet, keeping it moist. Place the green chiles, topped with cheese, on one half of omelet. Fold over and serve on a hot platter. Garnish with warmed - hot salsa. (serves 4)

SALSAS

(HOT SAUCES)

SALSA DE CHILE VERDE
GREEN CHILE SAUCE

10	green chile peppers
2	fresh tomatoes
1	medium onion
1/2 teaspoon	salt

Roast green chiles and peel. Cut up the chiles and mash. Mince onion and add to green chiles. Chop the tomatoes, add to green chiles and mix thoroughly. Add salt to taste.

Green chile salsa is especially good with broiled steak, short ribs and beans. (4 to 6 servings)

SALSA JALAPEÑA
JALAPEÑO SAUCE

1 16-oz.	canned tomatoes
1 1/2 teaspoon	salt
1	clove garlic
1 or 2	hot chile pepper (jalapeño, roasted and peeled)
1/4 cup	white vinegar
1 teaspoon	oregano

Place all the ingredients in a blender and blend briskly. Pour in a jar and store in the refrigerator. Will keep one week. (Yields 1 pint)

SALSA BRAVA DE CHILITOS AMARILLOS
HOT SAUCE WITH YELLOW PEPPERS

4	yellow peppers (minced)
2	white onions (minced)
1 28-oz.	can tomatoes
1 1/2 teaspoons	salt
1	garlic clove

Combine minced peppers and onions. Blend tomatoes with salt and garlic clove in a blender. Combine all ingredients in a saucepan and simmer 10 minutes. Stir once or twice. Pour into a glass jar, cover with lid, and refrigerate. This hot sauce is used with beans, carne asada and eggs. (Yields 2 pints)

SALSA DE TOMATE - BRAVA
HOT TOMATO SAUCE

1 16-oz.	canned tomatoes
1 clove	garlic
1 teaspoon	salt
4 or 6	chile tepins
1 teaspoon	oregano

Place all ingredients in blender and blend well. Transfer to a glass jar and refrigerate. Will keep for one week.

This sauce is delicious on tacos, tostadas, Spanish omelet and many other dishes. (Yields 1 pint)

SALSITA DE TOMATE FRESCO - PICANTE
FRESH TOMATO RELISH - HOT

3	fresh tomatoes, large (cubed)
1	jalapeño pepper, or 1 yellow hot; (finely chopped)
1/2 teaspoon	salt
1/8 teaspoon	garlic powder

Mix ingredients in the order listed and place in a covered jar. Store the relish in refrigerator. Use as needed for carne asada, barbecued steaks, beans, tacos, etc.

NOTE: Decrease amount of hot pepper to produce a mild relish (not so hot). (Yields 1 pint)

SALSA PICANTE DE TOMATE CON CEBOLLA
HOT TOMATO SAUCE WITH ONIONS

1 28-oz.	canned tomatoes
1 1/2 Teaspoon	salt
1	clove garlic
6	chile tepins
1 tablespoon	shortening
1 large	onion or 2 small
1	tablespoon flour

Blend tomatoes, salt, garlic and chiles in blender. Slice onions into thin slices. Melt shortening in a saucepan, sauté onion slices, then add flour and mix well until slightly brown. Add tomato mixture and allow to simmer for 10 minutes.

This sauce can be stored in refrigerator and used as needed. It can be used with chiles rellenos, with carne asada or broiled steaks. It can also be used as a dip with toasted corn tortilla chips. Just reheat. (Yields 2 pints)

Copyright Amalia Ruiz Clark, 1986

SALSA DE JALAPEÑOS ENCURTIDOS
PICKLED JALAPEÑO RELISH

15	fresh chile jalapeños (diced)
1	medium white onion (diced)
1/2 cup	white vinegar
1/2 cup	water
1 teaspoon	salt

Mix vinegar and water and bring to a boil; simmer 5 minutes. Allow to cool.

Dice jalapeños and onion. Mix. In a 16-oz. jar, place jalapeño mixture, add 1 teaspoon salt and over this pour the cooled vinegar (DO NOT STIR CONTENTS). Cover jar with lid and refrigerate. This will keep for several weeks.

This relish goes very good with broiled steak, refried beans and hamburger. Try it on a ham sandwich! (Yields 1 pint)

PEPINILLOS BRAVOS
HOT PICKLES

1 48-oz.	jar of whole kosher dill pickles
1	hot yellow pepper or jalapeño
8 to 10 oz.	white vinegar

Empty the jar of its contents, saving 1/2 the liquid. Cut pickles in half, lengthwise. Cut the pepper in quarters. Put the liquid, pepper and pickles in the jar and add the 8 to 10 ounces of white vinegar until jar is filled. Screw lid on as tightly as possible and store in the refrigerator. These will keep for several weeks.

Hot pickles can be used in sandwiches, ham, roast beef, cheese, and bean burritos. Also with hamburgers or as a zesty snack. (Yields 1 1/2 quarts)

SALSA DE FRUTA
FRUIT SALSA

2 cups	papaya chunks
2 cups	pineapple chunks
2 cups	mango chunks
1	green apple, peeled cored, and sliced
1/2 cup	red bell pepper, sliced
2 tablespoons	sugar
1/2 teaspoon	salt
1	jalapeño chile
1/2 cup	seaeoned rice vinegar
1/4 cup	fresh cilantro, minced

Mix all ingredients together and chill for 4 hours. (Serves 8)

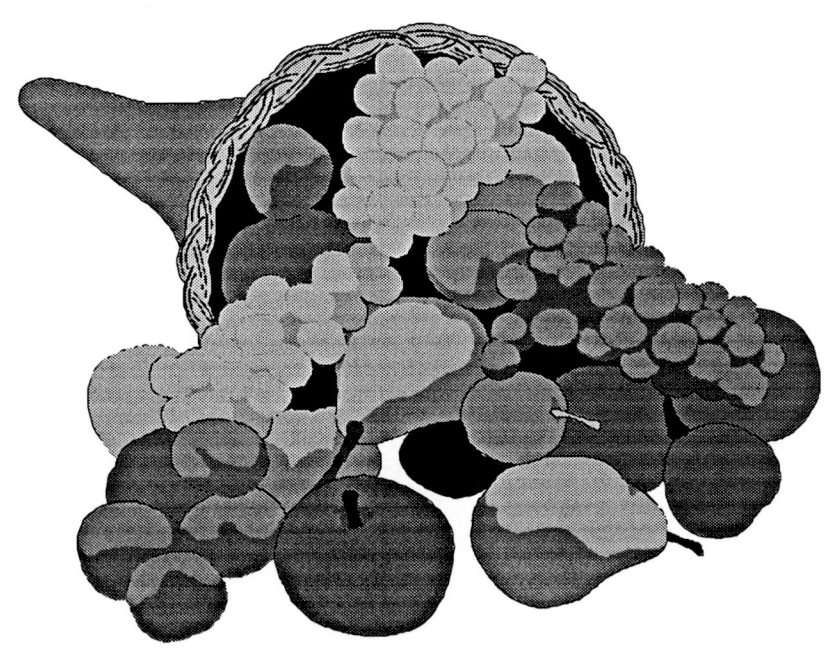

COPYRIGHT AMALIA RUIZ CLARK, 1986

LEGUMBRES

(VEGETABLES)

NOPALES
Prickly Pear Cactus

Prickly pear cactus is a native vegetable of Arizona; a vegetable that can be found in other Southwestern states, including Hawaii, and other countries as far off as Australia and the northern island of New Zealand. Prickly pear pads have thorns, but I can assure you, they are not that hard to clean. Only the young tender pads are picked for cooking. You will find them in abundance during the spring months. Prickly pear cactus is also grown domestically in Arizona. These pads have fewer thorns than the desert ones. The prickly pear pad is a delightful and nutritious vegetable, comparable to green beans or okra but with its unique flavor. Fresh nopal pads can be found at some supermarkets but are more commonly sold jarred or canned. This vegetable can be served plain or with red chile sauce, meats, eggs and salads. You will find delicious recipes using the nopal pads as a vegetable ingredient.

NOPALES
PRICKLY PEAR CACTUS
(BASIC RECIPE)

18	tender pads (approximately 5" in diameter or 3"x6" pads)
1/2 cup	salt
1/4 cup	white vinegar
1	onion
6	garlic cloves
8 quarts	water

TO PREPARE FOR COOKING: Place pad on small board holding it with fork and scraping with knife to remove thorns, holding the pad under running water. The rough outer skin will often peel off. Cut the pad in diagonal 1-inch strips and rinse in cold water. Parboil in 4 quarts of water. Add salt and vinegar. Skim foam until clear water remains. Cook 10 minutes. Drain and add the remaining 4 quarts of water. Add whole onion and garlic cloves. Cook for 10 minutes. Allow to cool, remove onion and garlic cloves and store in same water in refrigerator until ready to use. (Will keep 1 week). (Yields 4 quarts)

NOPALITOS CON CHORIZO
NOPALITOS WITH MEXICAN SAUSAGE

    2 cups   nopalitos (cooked and drained) use basic recipe
    2 cups   chorizo (see recipe)
2 tablespoons   shortening

Melt shortening in a skillet. Add chorizo and cook for 15 minutes turning it several times. Add nopalitos and mix thoroughly. Ready to eat plain, with tortilla or burrito style. (Serves 4)

NOPALITOS CON CHILE COLORADO
NOPALITOS WITH RED CHILE SAUCE

2 cups   nopalitos (cooked and drained) basic recipe or canned
2 cups   Prepared Red Chile Sauce (basic recipe)
1/2 cup   shredded jack cheese

Use 2 cups of Prepared Red Chile Sauce. Add nopalitos to the sauce. Allow to simmer in saucepan for 15 minutes then sprinkle shredded cheese. Remove from heat. Serve hot. (Serves 4)

NOPALITOS CON JAMÓN
NOPALITOS WITH HAM

2 cups	nopalitos (cooked and drained) see basic recipe
2 cups	ham (diced)
1/2 cup	green onions (chopped)
1/2 cup	bell pepper (chopped)
1 tablespoon	cooking oil
1/2 cup	jack cheese (shredded)
1/2 teaspoon	paprika

Heat the oil in a casserole and add all ingredients, except cheese and paprika. Mix thoroughly. Sprinkle cheese and paprika over mixture and bake in preheated oven at 400° for 15 minutes, or until cheese is melted. (Serves 4)

NOPALITOS CON CUAJADA
NOPALITOS WITH COTTAGE CHEESE

2 cups	cooked nopalitos with 1/4 cup liquid (basic recipe)
1 tablespoon	cooking oil
1 cup	cottage cheese

Heat oil in a skillet. Add nopalitos turning them frequently for about 1 minute. Add cottage cheese and continue turning the mixture until all cottage cheese is melted. Serve hot. (Serves 4)

GUISANTE
BLACK-EYED PEAS

1 pound	fresh black-eyed peas (shelled)
3 to 4 cups	water
1/2 teaspoon	salt
6	strips thick bacon (cut into 2 inch strips)
1/3 cup	green onion (minced)
1/4 cup	fresh cilantro (minced)

Place peas in a saucepan and add water and salt. Bring to a boil. Cover pan, lower heat and simmer for about 2 hours.

In a skillet, fry bacon until medium crisp. Add onion and cilantro (coriander) quickly and mix these ingredients into the peas. Simmer 25 minutes. Serve hot. Will freeze. (Serves 4)

CALABAZITAS CON ELOTE
ZUCCHINI WITH WHITE CORN

1 pound	zucchini (squash)
1 tablespoon	vegetable oil
1	fresh tomato (chopped)
1/2	onion (chopped)
1/2 teaspoon	salt
dash	black pepper
1 16-oz.	can (2 cups) white kernel corn and half the liquid
1/2 pound	cheese (Cheddar or jack)

Wash and trim squash. Cut into chunk size pieces. Place oil in 2-quart saucepan. Add squash and other ingredients. Bring to a boil, reduce heat and simmer for 20 minutes. Add cheese and simmer until cheese melts. (Serves 4 to 6)

Copyright Amalia Ruiz Clark, 1986

SPINACA
SPINACH

2 bunches	spinach
1/2 cup	water
1/2 teaspoon	salt
2 tablespoons	shortening or cooking oil
2	green onions (chopped)
1	tablespoon flour
dash	garlic powder

Clean spinach and wash thoroughly. Place in saucepan and add 1/2 cup water and salt. Cook slowly for 10 to 15 minutes or until tender. Chop spinach. In separate saucepan, heat oil, add onions and sauté. Add flour and brown lightly, then add greens and liquid. Add garlic powder. Give the spinach a few turns and let simmer for 5 minutes. For variations, add 1/2 cup cooked and drained whole beans, pinto or small red beans.

Kale, turnip tops, greens and mustard greens may be prepared in this manner. (Serves 4)

CALABAZA MEXICANA COSIDA
COOKED MEXICAN PUMPKIN

    1   Mexican pumpkin, or Butternut Squash
            (approximately 5 pounds)
    2 cups water

Wash the pumpkin, cut it and remove the seeds. Cut into medium size pieces. Place in a big pot, add the water, cover and cook at low heat for about 1 hour, or until tender. Let Cool. Scoop pumpkin pulp, place in a bowl and refrigerate or freeze. Cooked Mexican pumpkin is used for making "cajeta", a sweet pumpkin filling used in turnovers. (Yields 2 quarts)

ELOTE FRITO
FRIED CORN

    2 cups   corn kernels (take 4 or 5 ears of corn
                  and slice kernels off the cob)
    1 tablespoon shortening
    1/3 cup   onion (chopped)
    1   green pepper (chopped)
    1/2 teaspoon salt
    1/8 teaspoon black pepper
    1/2 teaspoon sugar
    1 1/2 cups   water

Heat shortening in a saucepan. Add onion and pepper. Sauté. Add corn and mix. Add water with seasonings, cover and simmer for 30 minutes, stirring occasionally until liquid is completely absorbed.

Canned corn kernels may be substituted. Use 1/2 cup of can liquid and simmer 15 minutes. (Serves 4)

CHILES RELLENOS
GREEN CHILES STUFFED WITH CHEESE

8 whole	green chiles (roasted and peeled or canned)
1 pound	Colby or jack cheese (cut into 2 inch strips)
1/2 cup	flour
1/2 teaspoon	salt
4	eggs
1 tablespoon	flour
1/2 cup	shortening

Mix 1/2 cup flour and 1/2 teaspoon salt together and set aside.

Make a slit on the chile pepper and stuff with a strip of cheese. Prepare all chiles this way and set aside.

Beat egg whites until stiff and slowly fold in flour. Beat egg yolks lightly and fold into the egg whites.

Roll stuffed chiles in flour. Dip only one stuffed chile at a time in the egg batter and quickly transfer the chile to skillet with moderately hot shortening. Several chiles rellenos can be cooked at the same time. Brown on each side and place on paper towel to drain. Garnish with Salsa Picante De Tomate Con Cebolla (see recipe). Serve hot. (Yields 8 chiles rellenos)

Variation- NOT FRIED! Roasted and peeled chiles poblanos stuffed with mozzerella cheese, mixed with white corn kernels. Pour chile poblano sauce over chiles. Garnish with corn kernels. Bake in oven till cheese melts. See recipe for chile poblano sauce.

CHAYOTES RELLENOS
STUFFED SQUASH

6 large	chayotes
	water to cover
1	garlic (minced)
1 teaspoon	salt
1 small	onion chopped
1 cup	corn kernels
2 tablespoon	butter
1/2 cup	Cheddar cheese (shredded)

Cut chayotes in half lengthwise. Cook chayotes in water in a large sauce pan. Cover and simmer for 35 to 40 minutes. Drain and cool. Carefuly scoop pulp, try not to tear shells, Set aside. In a skillet, melt butter. Add minced garlic, saute for 1 minute, stirring constantly. Add onion and saute until onions wilt but not brown, add corn kernels saute for 2 minutes. Add chayote pulp and simmer for 10 to 15 minutes. Spoon mixture into chayote shells, sprinkle tops with shredded cheese. Bake in a preheated oven a 350 degrees for 15 to 20 minutes or until cheese is melted. Garnish with cilantro sprigs. Serves 6. Note: Chayotes belongs to the squash family; sometimes called vegetable pears.

COPYRIGHT AMALIA RUIZ CLARK, 1986

POSTRES

(TRADITIONAL SWEETS)

ARROZ CON LECHE
RICE PUDDING

1 cup	rice (white)
2 cups	water
1/4 teaspoon	salt
1 piece	cinnamon stick (cut into 4 pieces)
1 cup	evaporated milk
3 cups	fresh milk
3/4 cup	sugar
3 large	eggs
	ground cinnamon

Place rice, water and salt in a large saucepan and bring to a boil. Stir once, cover pan, and simmer for 10 minutes. Add cinnamon pieces, milk and sugar. Bring to a boil, cover and simmer for 35 minutes. Separate egg yolks and save the whites for later. Beat the yolks until frothy, add to rice mixture, mix quickly, stirring constantly until mixture thickens. Remove from heat. Beat egg whites until stiff and fold gently into hot rice mixture. Pour into a large bowl and sprinkle with ground cinnamon. Serve warm or cold. (Serves 10)

BISCOCHUELOS
PASTRY RING COOKIE

4 cups	Masa Harina
1 teaspoon	salt
4 teaspoons	ground anise
1 1/4 cup	sugar
1 1/4	shortening
3	eggs (large)
1/4 cup	water

In large bowl, mix ingredients as listed, adding 1 teaspoon water at a time to mixture until dough sticks together (similar to pie dough). Take small amounts of dough, the size of a walnut, and roll between hands until dough is pencil thin. Bring ends together to shape a ring, overlapping the ends, and pinch together. Place on ungreased cookie sheet. Bake at 375° for approximately 10-12 minutes, or until pastry is light brown. (Yields approx. 4 dozen)

BUÑUELOS
MEXICAN CRULLERS

```
     3 cups    flour
1 teaspoon    salt
    1/4 cup    shortening & 1 cup warm water
1 1/2 cups    shortening for deep frying
```

Sift dry ingredients. Cut in 1/4 cup shortening and add water gradually until all water is absorbed. Knead mixture as for tortillas, until dough is smooth. Pat with shortening and let stand 20 minutes. Knead again. Divide dough into 12 balls the size of a golf ball. Pat each ball with shortening and let stand for 30 minutes. Proceed to make buñuelos like you would thin tortillas, or use a rolling pin to roll out. Deep fry each tortilla until golden brown on both sides. Drain on absorbent paper. A favorite way to eat buñuelos is to break one up in a bowl and serve with a trickle of Miel Para Buñuelos (see recipe following page).

This is a traditional New Year's favorite. (Yields 12)

CHURROS
MEXICAN CRULLERS

1 cup	flour
1/4 teaspoon	salt
1 cup	water (boiling)
1	egg (lightly beaten)
1 teaspoon	sherry wine
1 cup	cooking oil
	powdered sugar

Bring water to boiling point in a saucepan. Remove saucepan from fire and gradually add sifted flour with salt. Beat vigorously until fluffy and smooth. Add egg and wine and continue beating until batter is smooth and shiny. Heat oil in a deep pan until medium hot. Pour batter in a pastry tube and drop small amounts of batter about 4-5 inches long in the hot oil. Fry both sides until golden brown and remove churros to absorbent paper to drain. Roll each one in powdered sugar while still hot. This is a favorite pastry served with hot cocoa. (Yields 12)

MIEL PARA BUÑUELOS
BUÑUELO SYRUP

2 cups	crushed panocha or dark brown sugar
1 small	cinnamon stick
3 cups	water
2 tablespoons	maple syrup

Combine panocha or brown sugar, water, cinnamon stick and maple syrup in a saucepan. Bring to a boil and let simmer for 15 minutes or until syrup becomes medium thick.

Copyright Amalia Ruiz Clark, 1986

CAJETA PARA EMPANADAS
PUMPKIN FILLING FOR TURNOVERS

8 cups	cooked Mexican pumpkin
1 cup	brown sugar
1 cup	granulated sugar
2 tablespoons	ground cloves (coarse)
dash	salt

Mix ingredients in order. Simmer mixture for 3 1/2 hours, stirring frequently. Mixture should cook to a very thick consistency. Set aside to cool. Refrigerate and use when needed. (Yields 7 cups)

MASA PARA EMPANADAS
PASTRY FOR TURNOVERS

3 cups	flour
1/2 teaspoon	salt
3 tablespoons	sugar
1/2 cup	shortening
3/4 cup	cold water

Mix dry ingredients. Cut in the shortening and add water to hold dough together. Divide dough into 20 balls the size of a golf hall. Roll out and flatten the dough with a rolling pin on a floured board to about 6 inches in diameter.

Use one heaping tablespoon cooked fruit mixture on one-half of the rolled-out dough (avoid coming too close to the edges). Moisten edges with cold water. Fold half of the pastry over the fruit filling and press edges together to seal. Fry in a skillet or bake in preheated oven at 375° for 15 to 18 minutes, or until golden brown.

FRUIT FILLING FOR EMPANADAS: Use 2 cups of Cajeta Para Empanadas (see recipe). (Yields 20 Empanadas)

Copyright Amalia Ruiz Clark, 1986

CAPIROTADA
MEXICAN BREAD PUDDING

1 quart	water
2 cups	crushed panocha or brown sugar
6 whole	cloves
6 slices	French bread (toasted with butter and cubed 1" thick)
1 medium	apple (sliced)
1 cup	Raisins
1 cup	peanuts (salted or cashews)
1/2 pound	grated cheese (Monterey jack or longhorn)
1/4 cup	green onion tops (finely chopped)
1/4 cup	fresh cilantro (coriander) (finely chopped)

Boil water with cloves and brown sugar until syrupy (about 15 minutes). Arrange a layer of cubed bread in bottom of a buttered casserole. Cover with a layer of apples; sprinkle some raisins, cheese, peanuts, onions and cilantro. Repeat the layers until all ingredients are used. Remove cloves from syrup and pour syrup over ingredients in casserole dish. Bake in a preheated oven at 325° about 30 minutes. Serve either hot or cold.

This dessert is traditionally served during the Lenten season.

COYOTAS
BROWN SUGAR PASTRY

2 1/2 cups	crushed panocha or brown sugar
3 cups	flour
1/2 teaspoon	salt
1/2 cup	shortening
3/4 cup	cold water

Combine and mix dry ingredients. Cut in the shortening. Add water to hold dough together. Divide dough into 20 balls the size of a golf ball. Roll the ball of dough out with a rolling pin on a floured board to about 5 inches in diameter. Sprinkle about 2 tablespoons crushed panocha (or brown sugar) on one rolled out pastry. Moisten edges with cold water. Place another rolled out pastry on top and press edges together to seal. Bake in preheated oven at 375° for 15 minutes, or until golden brown. (Yields 10 coyotas)

PASTELITOS DE BODA
MEXICAN WEDDING CAKES

3/4 cup	butter
4 tablespoons	powdered sugar
1 tablespoon	cognac or brandy
1 teaspoon	cold water
2 cups	all-purpose flour
1 cup	pecans (finely chopped)
1 cup	powdered sugar (to roll pastelitos)

Cream butter until fluffy, add sugar, cognac and cold water. Mix thoroughly and add flour and nuts. Make into small balls and chill about 1 hour. Place on ungreased baking sheet and bake in preheated oven at 400 degrees for 10 minutes. Roll in powered sugar while hot. (Makes 4 dozen)

Copyright Amalia Ruiz Clark, 1986

PASTEL DE CAFE CON DATILES Y NUESES
DATE NUT COFFEE CAKE

1 pound	dates (pitted and chopped)
3 cups	strong coffee (boiling hot)
2 teaspoons	baking soda
3/4 cups	cooking oil
2 cups	sugar
2	eggs (lightly beaten)
4 cups	sifted flour
1/2 teaspoon	salt
1 tablespoon	vanilla
1 cup	chopped walnuts
6	candied cherries cut in half
6	shelled walnuts cut in half

Combine dates, hot coffee, baking soda and oil in a large mixing bowl. Let cool. Add sugar, eggs, flour, salt and vanilla. Mix thoroughly. Add walnuts and mix again. Pour cake batter in a greased and floured tubular cake pan. Decorate top of cake with cherries and walnuts. Bake in a preheated oven at 325° for 1 hour and 15 minutes. Test with a toothpick for doneness. (Yields 1 cake)

PASTEL DE OREJONES DE ALBARICOQUE
APRICOT PIE - DRIED APRICOTS

1 pound	dried apricots
2 cups	water
2/3 cup	sugar
1 tablespoon	cornstarch
2 tablespoons	water

Soak apricots for 20 minutes in a saucepan. Simmer in the same water for 20 minutes, mash lightly. Mix cornstarch with 2 tablespoons water and mix in with apricots, stirring constantly. Simmer 10 minutes or until thickened. Set aside to cool. To prepare pie crust see following recipe. (Yields 1 pie)

PASTA DE PASTEL
PIE CRUST

2 cups	sifted flour
2/3 cup	shortening
1/4 teaspoon	salt
3 tablespoons	cold water

Place sifted flour and salt in a mixing bowl. Cut in shortening with pastry blender until mixture becomes fine. Sprinkle cold water on mixture; mixing with pastry blender until mix is evenly dampened. Press pastry into 2 balls. Roll pastry 1/8 inch thick. Use one pie crust for the bottom and one for the top. Fit pie crust in a 9-inch pie pan. Fill with apricot fruit filling. Place top crust and cut slits to let steam out while baking. Trim top crust 1/2 inch larger than pan. Fold edges of top crust under bottom crust and press together with fork or fingers. Bake in a preheated oven at 425° for 45 minutes. (Yields 2 crusts)

Copyright Amalia Ruiz Clark, 1986

TAMALITOS DE LECHE DE MASA FRESCA
MINIATURE SWEET CORN MASA BALLS IN SWEET MILK SAUCE

2 cups	masa fresca
2 tablespoons	coarsely ground anise
2 tablespoons	sugar
1 tablespoon	water
3 cups	sweet milk (fresh or evaporated diluted to directions)
1/4 cup	sugar

Mix masa, anise, sugar, salt and water. Save 1/4 cup of mixture, add 2 tablespoons water and mix. Set aside. Mix 3 cups milk and sugar in a saucepan, bring to a boil, and lower the flame to keep mixture hot. Pinch a small piece of masa, form into a small ball the size of a marble, flatten middle with thumb, and drop it into hot milk. Continue this process until all the masa has been used. Simmer 20 minutes, stirring constantly to keep milk from sticking or burning on bottom of pan. Add the 1/4 cup mixture saved earlier and mix quickly, continue to simmer until thickened (about 5 minutes). Pour in a bowl and cover. May be served warm or cold. Refrigerate or freeze. (Serves 6)

TAMALITOS DE LECHE DE MASA HARINA
MINIATURE SWEET MASA HARINA BALLS IN SWEET MILK SAUCE

1 cup	Masa Harina
4 tablespoons	sugar
2 tablespoons	anise (coarsely ground)
1 cup	water
3 cups	sweet milk (fresh or evaporated diluted to directions)
1/4 cup	sugar

Mix Masa Harina, sugar and anise. Add the water and mix thoroughly. Set aside. Save 1/4 cup of mixture, add 2 tablespoons water and mix. Set aside.

TO COOK: Follow same instructions for recipe Tamalitos De Leche De Masa Fresca. (Serves 4)

FLAN
CARAMEL COATED CUSTARD

2/3 cup	sugar
3/4 cup	sugar
4 cups	half and half (fresh cream and milk)
4	eggs
1 stick	cinnamon
1	fresh lemon peel
9 tablespoons	Kahlua liqueur or rum

TO PREPARE CARAMEL COATING: Melt 2/3 cup sugar in small saucepan over low heat, stirring constantly until caramel syrup turns light golden brown (about 15 minutes). Pour caramel syrup into a 1 1/2-quart mold or baking dish and swirl to coat bottom and sides. Set aside.

TO PREPARE CUSTARD: Mix 3/4 cup sugar, half and half cream, cinnamon stick, lemon peel, and 6 tablespoons Kahlua or rum in a saucepan. Heat mixture over low heat and simmer for 5 minutes, stirring constantly. Remove from heat, set aside and allow to cool about 10 minutes. Remove cinnamon stick and lemon peel. Beat eggs until frothy in a large bowl, add to milk mixture and mix well. Pour into mold.

Bake in shallow baking pan containing 2 inches boiling water, in preheated oven at 350° for 60 minutes, or until custard is firm. Remove from baking pan and cool to lukewarm. Cover and refrigerate until cool.

TO SERVE: Loosen flan around edge with knife. Place in rimmed serving dish upside down over mold. Holding mold and dish, turn together so dish is upright and lift. Caramel will flow out to form sauce. For flaming dessert pour 3 tablespoons warm Kahlua over flan just before serving and ignite. (Serves 8)

FLAN DE MERENGUE
MERINGUE FLAN

12	egg whites
1/2 teaspoon	cream of tartar
1/8 teaspoon	salt
3/4 cup	sugar
1/4 cup	Kahlua
1/2 cup	toasted coconut, for topping

CARAMEL

1 1/2 cups	sugar
1/4 cup	Kahlua

To prepare caramel: Melt 1 1/2 cups of sugar in a non-stick skillet over low heat, stirring constantly until syrup turns a golden brown. Pour syrup into a 2 quart bundt pan and swirl to coat bottom and sides of mold. Set aside.

Beat egg whites in a large bowl, add cream of tartar and salt. Beat egg whites until egg whites form stiff peaks. Gradually beat sugar into egg whites and add the Kahula. Pour meringue mixture into the caramel coated mold. Set the mold in a baking pan of 2 inchs of boiling water, and bake in a preheated oven at 350 F for 50 minutes. Turn oven off and let mold stand in oven for 10 minutes with oven door slightly open. Carefully remove mold and place it away from drafts. Let mold cool for 1/2 hour, unmold flan on an inverted platter and cover with more caramel sauce. Remove the rest of caramel from the mold by adding 1 cup of hot water and placing it in a 400 F oven for 10 minutes, or until syrupy. Add 1/4 cup Kahlua to caramel, let cool. Pour on flan. Top flan with toasted coconuts.

This is a light version of flan. (Serves 8)

CAJETA DE MEMBRILLO
QUINCE PASTE

    8   ripe quince (cored and cut in quarters)
4 cups   sugar

Put quince in a pot and cover with water. Cook at low heat for 25 minutes or until tender. Drain quinces (save some liquid) puree in blender, use a little liquid to facilitate blending.

Use 1 cup sugar for each cup of puree quince. Combine puree quince with sugar in a large saucepan and mix well. Bring to a boil and simmer. Use a wooden spoon to stir constantly so mixture won't burn. Cook mixture until it thickens and bottom of pan can be seen when spoon is drawn across it (about 1 hour). Remove from heat, let mixture cool to lukewarm stirring frequently. Pour into small buttered molds and let stand until it hardens. Unmold to serve. Serve for dessert, with cheese or meats. Store in refrigerator or freeze. (Yields approx. 3 cups)

JAMONCILLO
MEXICAN FUDGE

  2 cups   milk
  2 cups   sugar
  1 stick   cinnamon
1/3 cup   chopped nuts (walnuts, pecans or peanuts)
              additional nuts in halves for decorations

Combine milk, sugar and cinnamon stick in a saucepan. Bring to a boil and boil on low heat. Stir frequently with a wooden spoon until mixture thickens or until bottom of pan can be seen when spoon is drawn across it (about 1 hour cooking time). Remove cinnamon stick. Stir in nuts.

Pour candy quickly into small buttered molds lined with a decorative pattern of nuts. Custard cups or tiny loaf pans may be used. Let candy cool thoroughly, then turn candy out of molds. Cut in small individual pieces if desired.

To make individual candies, cool mixture just enough to be handled. Butter hands and roll spoonful of candy between palms into a small ball. Press a half nut into top of ball. Place on a buttered cookie sheet or wax paper to cool. This is a traditional sweet. (Yields 30 individual candies)

PEPITORIA
PUMPKIN SEED CANDY

1 pound	panocha (piloncillo)
1/2 cup	water
1 cup	shelled pumpkin seeds

In a large saucepan combine panocha and water. Cook on low heat, stirring frequently with a wooden spoon. Cook to a medium ball stage, about 245° on candy thermometer. Quickly stir in shelled pumpkin seeds. Working very fast, drop a spoonful of mixture on a buttered baking sheet and flatten with a spoon to 2" circle.

NOTE: Panocha is unrefined brown Mexican sugar sold in little pillars, usually found in Mexican stores or delicatessen food shops. Shelled pumpkin seeds can be bought in health food shops and some drug stores. (Yields 35 candies)

MOUSSE DE KAHLUA
KAHLUA MOUSSE

1 cup	heavy whipping cream, chilled
1 teaspoon	instant expresso coffee powder
1/4 cup	Kahlua
2 tablespoons	sugar
1	egg white
2 teaspoons	sugar
	Chocolate shavings
	Rasberries, fresh or frozen

Beat whipping cream and coffee in a chilled bowl using ice cold beaters. Beat until stiff. Add Kahlua and 2 tablespoons of sugar. Beat until very stiff. In a small bowl beat egg white until soft peaks form. Add 2 teaspoons of sugar and beat until stiff. Fold egg white into whipped cream mixture. Cover and chill. Scrve in dessert glasses and decorate with chocolate shavings and 3 or 4 rasberries. (Serves 6)

COPYRIGHT AMALIA RUIZ CLARK, 1986

ALMENDRADO
ALMOND PUDDING

1 1/2 envelopes	Gelatin
1/2 cup	cold water
1/2 cup	boiling water
6	egg whites
1/2 cup	sugar
1/2 teaspoon	vanilla
1/2 teaspoon	almond extract
	Red and green food coloring

Soak gelatin in cold water. Add boiling water to dissolve. Cool. Beat egg whites stiff, but not dry. Gradually add the sugar, alternating with the gelatin liquid, using an electric beater at high speed. Add vanilla and almond. Be sure to whip thoroughly so the gelatin blends completely with the egg whites.

Divide the mixture into three parts, leaving one part white. Tint the others red and green to resemble the Mexican flag. Alternate layers by spooning into a loaf pan lined with waxed paper which extends above the mixture. Chill at least 4 hours and serve with the following custard.

NATILLAS DE ALMENDRADO
ALMOND CUSTARD

2 tablespoons	cornstarch
1 tablespoon	cold milk
3 cups	scalded milk
1/2 cup	sugar
3/4 cup	chopped almonds
6	egg yolks
1/2 teaspoon	vanilla
1/2 teaspoon	almond extract
	Sliced, toasted almonds

Dissolve cornstarch in cold milk, add to scalded milk, sugar and salt. Boil until slightly thickened, stirring constantly. Beat egg yolks, vanilla and almond extracts. Slowly add to hot mixture. Stir constantly until slightly thickened (about 1 minute). Add almonds and stir. Chill. To serve: slice almendrado and top with the custard sauce and garnish with toasted almonds. (Serves 8)

PAN DULCE
SWEET BREAD

1 cake	rapid rise yeast
1/2 cup	warm water
1 tablespoon	sugar
3 1/2 cups	sifted all purpose flour
2 tablespoon	margarine, melted
1/2 cup	sugar
2	eggs, beaten

TOPPING:

1/2 cup	sugar
1/4 cup	margarine
1/4 teaspoon	salt
1 teaspoon	cinnamon
1	egg yolk
2/3 cup	sifted flour

Add yeast, salt, sugar and margarine to warm water, stir well, add 1/2 of flour and cover. Place in a warm spot until it doubles in size. Punch down, add beaten eggs and rest of flour. Cover and let rise again until double in size. Knead for 5 minutes, roll out on floured board, divide into 12 pieces and form into round buns.

Topping for buns:

Cream sugar, margarine, salt and cinnamon until well blended. Add egg yolk and flour and stir until crumbly mixture is formed. Spread topping on each bun. Cover and let rise double in size. Bake at 400° F for 15 minutes. Sweet buns are great with coffee or hot chocolate. Have them for brunch. (Makes 12 buns)

INDEX

Adorno De Crema Agria Para Ensalada (Sour Cream Dressing) 91
Adorno De Vinagre Para Ensalada (Vinegar Salad Dressing) 92
Almendrado (Almond Pudding)..135
Aperitivo Bravo De Aguacate (Peppery Avocado Dip) 12
Aperitivo De Aguacate (Avocado Dip) 11
Aperitivo De Frijol (Mexican Bean Dip Fondue) 10
Aperitivo De Frijol Con Chile Jalapeño (Jalapeño Bean Dip) 10
Aperitivo De Jicama Fresca (Fresh Jicama Appetizer) 14
Arroz A La Espanola (Spanish Rice) 39
Arroz Con Leche (Rice Pudding) 119
Asado (Mexican Roast Beef)..23

Bebida De Pinole (Pinole Drink)...18
Biscochuelos (Pastry-Ring Cookies) 120
Bunuelos (Mexican Crullers) 121
Burrito Minero (Miners' Burrito) 26
Burritos De Carne Con Chile Verde (Green Chile Beef Burritos) 28
Barbacoa (Barbecued Spare Ribs - Pork) 27

Cajeta De Membrillo (Quince Paste)...132
Cajeta Para Empanadas (Pumpkin Filling For Turnovers) 123
Calabazitas Con Elote (Zucchini With White Corn) 113
Calabaza Mexicana Cosida (Cooked Mexican Pumpkin) 115
Caldo De Queso (Cheese Soup)..83
Capirotada (Mexican Bread Pudding) 124
Camaron Con Chiles Y Ajos (Chilled Shrimp in Garlic) 11
Carne Asada A La Mexicana (Tri-Tip Loin Roast in Chile Marinade) 44
Carne De Puerco Adobada (Marinated Spiced Pork Loin) 25
Carne Seca (Jerky-Basic Recipe) 23
Carne Seca Machacada Con Chile Colorado (Shredded Jerky With Chile Sauce)...24
Carne Seca Machacada Guisada (Shredded Jerky - Fried) 24
Casuela De Carne Seca Machacada (Shredded Jerky Soup) 84
Ceveche (Marinated Fish) 16
Chayotes Rellenos (Stuffed Squash) 117
Chilaquiles (Corn Tortilla Hash) 51
Chile Colorado Con Queso (Red Chile Sauce With Cheese) 61
Chile Con Carne - Guisado (Meat In Red Chile Puree) 61
Chile Con Carne Para Tamales (Chile Con Carne For Tamales) 64
Chimichangas (Deep Fried Meat Burro)..29
Chile Rellenos (Green Chiles Stuffed With Cheese) 116
Chocolate Mexicano (Mexican Chocolate)..18
Chocolate Con Kahlua (Chocolate With Kahlua) 19
Chorizo (Mexican Hot Sausage) 30

Chuletas De Puerco Con Chile Verde (Pork Chops With Green Chile) 26
Churros (Mexican Crullers) 122
Coctel De Abulon (Abalone Cocktail) 13
Corona De Puerco Asada Con Arroz (Roast Crown of Pork with Rice) 41
Costillas De Puerco Asadas Con Salsa De Barbacoa (Barbecued Spare Ribs) 27
Coyotas (Brown Sugar Pastry) 125
Cucharetas De Tortilla De Maiz (Corn Tortilla Chips) 47

Dulces Jamoncillo (Mexican Fudge) 132

Ejotes Con Chile Colorado (Green Beans With Prepared Red Chile Sauce) 40
Elote Frito (Fried Corn) 115
Empanadas Fritas (Fried Turnovers) 59
Enchiladas 53
Ensalada De Arandano (Cranberry Salad Mold) 89
Ensalada De Fruta Fresca (Fresh Fruit Salad) 90
Ensalada De Papaya Y Ciruela (Papaya Plum Salad) 90
Ensalada De Aguacate (Avocado Salad) 91
Ensalada De Nopalitos (Nopalitos Salad) 92
Ensalada De Camaron (Shrimp Salad) 93
Ensalada De Noche Buena (Christmas Eve Salada) 96
Ensalada De Papa (Potato Salad) 94
Ensalada De Salpicon (Beef Tongue Salad) 95

Fajitas En Escabechi De Tiquilla (Meat Strips Marinated in Tiquilla) 43
Flan (Caramel Coated Custard) 130
Flan De Meregue (Merigue Flan) 131
Frijoles Pintos (Pinto Beans - Basic Recipe) 72
Frijoles Fritos (Fried Beans) 73
Friioles Refritos (Refried Beans) 73
Frijoles Refritos Al Horno (Refried Beans-Baked) 73
Frijoles Fritos Con Chiles (Beans With Red Chile Peppers) 74
Frijoles Con Chile (Mexican Chile Beans) 74
Frijoles Con Carne (Beans With Meat) 74

Galletas De Zucchini (Tiny Zucchini Biscuits) 14
Gallina En Pipian (Chicken In Pipian Sauce) 32
Gorditas De Maiz De Masa Fresca (Homemade Corn Tortillas) 46
Gorditas De Masa Harina (Homemade Corn Tortillas) 47
Guajolote O Gallina Con Chile Colorado
    (Turkey or Chicken With Red Chile Sauce) 32
Guisante (Black-eyed Peas) 113
Guacamole (Basic Avocado Spread) 12
Huachinango A La Veracruzana (Red Snapper Veracruz Style) 42
Huevos Rancheros (Ranch Style Eggs) 98

Huevos Revueltos Con Carne Seca Machacada
  (Eggs Scrambled With Shredded Jerky) 99
Huevos Revueltos Con Chorizo (Scrambled Eggs With Hot Sausage) 100
Huevos Revueltos Con Nopalitos (Scrambled Eggs With Nopalitos) 99
Huevos Revueltos Con Papas (Scrambled Eggs With Potatoes) 100
Huevos Revueltos Con Tortillas Tostadas (Scrambled Eggs With Tortilla Chips) ...101
Huevos A La Benedict En Tortitas De Masa (Eggs Benedict On Masa Patties)......98

Jalapeños En Escabeche Rellenos Con Queso
  (Pickled Jalapeños Stuffed With Cheese) 15

Macarron Con Chile Colorado (Macaroni With Red Chile Sauce) 39
Masa Para Empanadas (Pastry For Turnovers)..123
Menudo (Tripe Soup) 86
Miel Para Bunuelos (Bunuelo Syrup) 122
Mole Poblano (Poblano Sauce) 62
Mousse De Kahlua (Kahlua Mousse) 134

Natilas De Almendrado (Almond Custard) 136
Nixtamal (Mexican Hominy)...45
Nopales (Prickly Pear Cactus) 109
Nopalitos 111

Pan Dulce (sweet Bread) 137
Pasta De Chile Colorado (Red Chile Puree) 60
Pasta De Chile Colorado - Guisado (Prepared Red Chile Sauce) 60
Pasta De Pastel (Pie Crust)..127
Pastel De Cafe Con Datiles Y Nueses (Date Nut Coffee Cake)....................126
Pastel De Chile Con Carne De Masa Fresca (Tamale Pie) 67
Pastel De Chile Con Carne De Masa Harina (Tamale Pie) 68
Pastel De Elote (Green Corn Tamale Pie) 70
Pastel De Orejones De Albaricoque (Apricot Pie - Dried Apricots) 127
Pasteliots De Boda (Mexican Wedding Cakes) 125
Pepinillos Bravos (Hot Pickles) 106
Pepitoria (Pumpkin Seed Candy) 133
Picadillo (Mexican Hash) 32
Picadillo De Lengua (Beef Tongue Hash) 33
Pierna De Catnero A La Mexicana (Leg of Lamb Mexican Style) 40
Pinole De Trigo (Roasted Ground Wheat Powder) 20
Pollo Asado Con Arroz (Baked Chicken With Rice)......................................35
Ponche (Mexican Eggnog) 19
Posole (Beans, Hominy and Pork Hocks) 75
Puchero (Mexican Stew) 85

Quesadillas De Tortillas De Maiz (Grilled Cheese Corn Tortillas) 48

Red Chile Sauce 61
Relleno De Arroz (Rice Stuffing) 35
Relleno Para Guajolte A La Mexicana (Turkey Stuffing, Mexican Style)............36

Salsa Brava De Chilitos Amarillos (Hot Sauce With Yellow Peppers) 104
Salsa De Barbacoa (Barbecue Sauce) 27
Salsa De Chile Verde (Green Chile Sauce) 103
Salsa De Fruta (Fruit Salsa)............107
Salsa De Jalapeños Encurtidos (Pickled Jalapeño Relish) 106
Salsa De Tomate - Brava (Hot Tomato Sauce) 104
Salsita De Tomate Fresco - Picante (Fresh Tomato Relish - Hot) 105
Salsa Jalapena (Jalapeño Sauce)............103
Salsa Picante De Tomate Con Cebolla (Hot Tomato Sauce With Onions) 105
Sopa De Albondigas (Mexican Meat Ball Soup) 79
Sopa De Lentejas (Lentil Soup) 80
Sopa De Fideo (Vermicelli Soup) 81
Sopa De Frijoles Negro Con Lentejas (Black Bean and Lentil Soup) 80
Sopa De Pollo (Chicken Soup) 82
Sopa De Tortilla (Tortilla Soup) 87
Spinaca (Spinach) 114
Sopapillas (Bread Puffs) 77

Tacos De Carne (Beef Tacos) 49
Tamales De Chile Con Carne De Masa Fresca (Red Chile Beef Tamales)............65
Tamales De Chile Con Carne De Masa Harina (Red Chile Beef Tamales)............66
Tamales De Elote (Green Corn Tamales) 68
Tamales De Frijol De Masa Fresca (Bean Tamales) 71
Tamales De Frijol De Masa Harina (Bean Tamales) 72
Tamalitos De Leche De Masa Fresca
   (Miniature Sweet Corn Masa Balls In Sweet Milk Sauce) 128
Tamalitos De Leche De Masa Harina
   (Miniature Sweet Masa Harina Balls in Sweet Milk Sauce)............129
Teswin (Fiesta Punch) 21
Torta De Carne Molida (Mexican Meat Loaf)............37
Tortillas 76
Tortillas De Maiz Para Tacos Blandos (Soft Tacos) 49
Tortitas De Camaron (Little Shrimp Omelets) 38
Tostadas De Frijoles (Bean Tostadas) 51
Tostada De Queso (Cheese Crisp) 13
Tortilla De Huevos Con Chile Verde (Green Chile Omelet) 101

Variedad De Rellenos Para Tacos (Variety Of Fillings For Tacos) 50

GIVE
Amillia's
SPECIAL MEXICAN DISHES
TO A FRIEND!

Just send a check or money order for $9.95 for each copy and $2.50 for postage and handling to:

Gila River Designs
P.O. Box 124
Oracle, Arizona 85623
(602) 896-2395

Please fill in shipping instructions below.

Name _____
Address _____
City _____ State _____ Zip _____

GIVE
Amillia's
SPECIAL MEXICAN DISHES
TO A FRIEND!

Just send a check or money order for $9.95 for each copy and $2.50 for postage and handling to:

Gila River Designs
P.O. Box 124
Oracle, Arizona 85623
(602) 896-2395

Please fill in shipping instructions below.

Name _____
Address _____
City _____ State _____ Zip _____

GIVE
Amillia's
SPECIAL MEXICAN DISHES
TO A FRIEND!

Just send a check or money order for $9.95 for each copy and $2.50 for postage and handling to:

Gila River Designs
P.O. Box 124
Oracle, Arizona 85623
(602) 896-2395

Please fill in shipping instructions below.

Name _____
Address _____
City _____ State _____ Zip _____

GIVE
Amillia's
SPECIAL MEXICAN DISHES
TO A FRIEND!

Just send a check or money order for $9.95 for each copy and $2.50 for postage and handling to:

Gila River Designs
P.O. Box 124
Oracle, Arizona 85623
(602) 896-2395

Please fill in shipping instructions below.

Name _____
Address _____
City _____ State _____ Zip _____